WARREN G. HARDING
1865-1923

Chronology—Documents—Bibliographical Aids

Edited by

PHILIP R. MORAN

Series Editor

HOWARD F. BREMER

1970

OCEANA PUBLICATIONS, INC.

Dobbs Ferry, New York

Library of Congress Catalog Card Number: 78-95013
Standard Book Number: 379-12064-X

Manufactured in the United States of America

CONTENTS

EDITOR'S FOREWORD

Every attempt has been made to cite the most accurate dates in this Chronology. Diaries, documents, and similar evidence have been used to determine the exact date. If, however, later scholarship has found such dates to be obviously erroneous, the more plausible date has been used. Should this Chronology be in conflict with other authorities, the student is urged to go back to original sources.

This is a research tool compiled primarily for the student. While it does make some judgments on the significance of the events, it is hoped that they are reasoned judgments based on a long acquaintance with American history.

Obviously, the very selection of events by any writer is itself a judgment.

The essence of these little books is in their making available some pertinent facts and key documents plus a critical bibliography which should direct the student to investigate for himself additional and/or contradictory material. Because the bulk of works about Harding was written during his last years and those immediately following his death, many may not always be available in small libraries. Documents in this volume are taken from the **Congressional Record.**

CHRONOLOGY

EARLY LIFE AND CAREER

1865

November 2   Born: Blooming Grove (Corsica), Ohio. Father: George T.: Mother: Phoebe Dickerson.

1873

Family moved to Caledonia, Ohio, where father practiced homeopathy. Harding worked as printer's devil on the Caledonia *Argus,* a weekly newspaper in which his father had a part interest.

1879

Began studies at Ohio Central College in Iberia. He played alto horn and edited school publication.

1882

Graduated from Ohio Central. Taught one term, from autumn until February, 1883, at a one-room school near Marion, to which his family had moved in 1882. Briefly studied law, sold insurance and was a reporter on Col. James H. Vaughn's *Mirror,* a Democratic weekly. Played in and managed the Marion Citizens Cornet Band.

1884

November 26   Published first issue of Marion *Star,* a previously bankrupt daily bought by Harding and two friends, John Sickel and Jack Warwick. Harding later became sole owner. Battled often in print with George Crawford, publisher-editor of the weekly *Independent,* a third Marion newspaper.

1891

July 8   Married Florence Kling DeWolfe, a divorcee five years older than himself, at Marion. Her father, wealthy Marion banker Amos Kling, objected to his son-in-law and often repeated the long-lasting, but unproven, claim that there was Negro blood in the Harding family. Mrs. Harding, firm and shrewd, managed business aspects of the *Star.* Among newsboys was Norman Thomas, the socialist.

1892

November   Beaten as token Republican candidate for county auditor.

1899

November 6   Elected Ohio state senator. During campaign, met Harry Micajah Daugherty at Richwood, Ohio, rally. Daugherty was to become a close political associate and Attorney General in his Cabinet.

1901

November   Reelected to Ohio senate. Was named Republican floor leader, and became popular speaker, known for his flowing style.

1903

November 3   Elected lieutenant governor of Ohio.

1905

Unsuccessful in hopes for Republican nomination for governorship, he devoted major attention to editing the *Star*. It was about this time that he met Carrie Phillips, wife of a friend, and initiated a love affair of many years' duration.

1909

Started profit-sharing plan, among first in Ohio, for *Star* employees.

1910

May 20   Mother died after injury in a fall.

November 8   Defeated as Republican candidate for governor by Judson Harmon, Democrat. Met schoolgirl Nan Britton about this time. Her father was a Marion physician.

1911

June 19   Attended with Mrs. Harding the silver wedding reception in Washington, D.C., of President and Mrs. Taft. Harding was a Taft supporter.

Summer   Carrie Phillips left Marion for a stay in Berlin that would last three years.

1912

June 18   Nominated William H. Taft for second term at stormy Chicago convention of the Republican party. Senator Elihu Root was chairman. In resulting split, Theodore

Roosevelt formed the Progressive Party in August, leading to victory of the Democratic candidate for the Presidency, Woodrow Wilson.

1914

August 11 In primaries, defeated Joseph B. Foraker for Republican nomination for United States senator. Foraker, a former senator, had lost 1909 bid for seat after his close ties with the Standard Oil Co. had been exposed.

Carrie Phillips returned from Germany that summer and resumed affair with Harding. Her pro-German sentiments were later to bring her under Secret Service surveillance.

1915

December 6 Took seat in Senate. Bought home on Wyoming Avenue. Undistinguished Senate service included membership on Commerce Committee. Associates included Ohioans Nicholas Longworth, senator, and Ned McLean, Cincinnati *Enquirer* publisher, and Senator Albert B. Fall of New Mexico.

1916

June 7-10 Delivered anti-Wilson keynote speech and was chairman at Republican national convention in Chicago. Charles Evans Hughes was nominated to run against Wilson. Harding had been considered a dark horse possibility for nomination.

1917

April 4 Harding spoke in favor of war with Germany, which was declared two days later.

That spring, Harding and Nan Britton began close relationship, with weekly meetings, that was to continue through most of his period as President.

December 3 The 65th Congress opened. As senator, Harding voted for war bills, Espionage Bill and Prohibition Amendment.

1918

November 5 Republicans gained control of both houses of Congress when voters rejected Wilson policies.

November 29 Chided Daugherty, in first of an exchange of letters, for intra-party political opposition to Harding. The two were not closely associated at this time.

1919

January 6   Death of Theodore Roosevelt helped push Harding into position of Ohio's "favorite son." At this time, though, Harding discouraged efforts to get him Republican nomination.

May 19   Named to Foreign Relations Committee in 66th Congress.

June 4   Suffrage Amendment sent to states for ratification. Harding supported it.

Summer-Fall   Harding's supporters, including Daugherty and Senator Boies Penrose of Pennsylvania, encouraged him to seek nomination. Meanwhile, a strong campaign was being mounted for candidate Gen. Leonard Wood.

September 11 In Senate speech, backed Henry C. Lodge in opposition to League of Nations.

September 26 President Wilson suffered a stroke following speech the previous day at Pueblo, Colorado, on national tour to gain support for League.

October 2   Nan Britton gave birth to a daughter, Elizabeth Ann. Harding was claimed to be the father.

November   Voted in Senate against League.

December 16   Declared himself as candidate for the Presidency. Daugherty, who had worked hard to persuade Harding, became his political manager.

1920

March 19   League ratification defeated in Senate.

May 5-10   Socialist Labor Party at national convention in New York City nominated William W. Cox of St. Louis for Presidency and August Gillhaus of Brooklyn for Vice Presidency.

May 8-14   Socialist Party meeting in New York City nominated Eugene V. Debs of Indiana for a fifth try for the Presidency. His running mate was Seymour Stedman of Ohio. Debs at the time was serving a 10-year sentence for wartime violation of the Espionage Act.

May 21	In Senate, the Kenyon Committee was appointed at the insistence of William Borah to investigate candidates' spending. The committee found that Wood had spent a recorded minimum of 1.75 million dollars.
May 27	Gave speech in Boston advocating "not nostrums but normalcy."
June 5	Poll by *Literary Digest* put Harding sixth as potential GOP nominee.
June 8	Republican convention opened in Chicago. Lodge was chairman.
June 11	After four ballots, top candidates Wood, Frank O. Lowden and Hiram Johnson were deadlocked. In Blackstone Hotel suite that night Harding was picked by an inner group including Senators Lodge, Frank B. Brandegee, James W. Wadsworth, Joseph M. McCormick and Joseph E. Grundy. This was the so-called "smoke-filled room," recalling Daugherty prediction early in year that Harding would be picked, after a ballot deadlock, by 15 or 20 men at 2:11 a.m.
June 12	Harding nominated on 10th ballot. The group of leaders had selected Irvine L. Lenroot of Wisconsin to be his running mate. However, the delegates, eager to get out of hot Chicago, voted for Calvin Coolidge, who had been nominated in a loud voice by Wallace McCamant, Oregon delegate.
	Brandegee termed Harding "the best of the second-raters." Harding himself said, "We drew to a pair of deuces and filled," referring to his unlikely success.
June 28-July 5	In San Francisco, Democrats nominated on the 44th ballot Ohio Governor James M. Cox to oppose Harding. Franklin Delano Roosevelt was his running mate.
July 13-16	Farmer-Labor Party at its first national convention, in Chicago, nominated Parley P. Christensen of Utah and Maximilian S. Hayes of Ohio as its candidates.
July 21-22	In Lincoln, Nebraska, the Prohibition Party convention

nominated Aaron S. Watkins of Ohio and David L. Colvin of New York as a national team.

July 22   Honored at Notification Day ceremonies in Marion.

August 26   Prohibition went into effect as Tennessee became 36th ratifying state.

August 28   In Marion speech, Harding affirmed his opposition to United States participation in the League of Nations. Harding conducted a "front porch" campaign, remaining mostly in Marion. His campaign slogan was "a return to normalcy." Cox and Roosevelt toured the country backing Wilson's policies.

Claims that Harding had Negro blood were circulated during the campaign, based primarily on writings of a biased college professor, William Estabrook Chancellor.

October 14   In move to gain support of those who favored United States membership in the League of Nations, a group of top pro-League Republicans publicly endorsed Harding as the best means to this end, despite his stated opposition to the League.

November 2   Elected President by a landslide vote, over 60%. Received 16,152,200 votes to Cox's 9,147,353; 404 electoral votes to Cox's 127; and won 37 of the 48 states. Republicans extended their majorities in both houses of Congress.

November 6   Began vacation trip to Texas, the Canal Zone and Jamaica.

December 4   Returned to country, landing at Norfolk.

December 5   Gave final speech as Senator at opening of session of Congress. He then returned to his home in Marion, where he conferred with many visitors who included Herbert Hoover, Hughes, Root and Taft.

1921

January 9   Resigned Senate seat.

January   In late January and February, he vacationed in Florida on houseboat of Senator Joseph S. Frelinghuysen of New Jersey. Visited William Jennings Bryan. Ended trip in St.

Augustine, where he completed and announced Cabinet selections.

February 27   Left St. Augustine.

TERM IN OFFICE

March 4   Sworn in as President on east portico of Capitol by Chief Justice Edward D. White. Accompanied to Capitol by President Wilson in automobile (this was first use of an automobile at an inauguration). A vague inaugural address stressed a "return to normalcy." There was no official ball or parade.

Cabinet members approved: Charles E. Hughes of New York, State; Andrew W. Mellon of Pennsylvania, Treasury; Henry C. Wallace of Iowa, Agriculture; Herbert C. Hoover of California, Commerce; Will H. Hays of Indiana, Postmaster General; John W. Weeks of Massachusetts, War; Harry M. Daugherty of Ohio, Attorney General; Albert B. Fall of New Mexico, Interior; Edwin Denby of Michigan, Navy; and James J. Davis of Pennsylvania, Labor.

April 11   Special session of Congress called by Harding opened.

April 12   In special message to Congress, Harding urged end of technical state of war, cutting of taxes, reduction of spending to cut war debts, enactment of tariff laws, creation of a national budget system and lower railroad rates.

Joint Agricultural Inquiry Commission created by Congress to investigate current conditions.

April 19   Accepted statue of Simon Bolivar in New York City as gift to the United States from Venezuela.

April 20   Senate approved a treaty with Colombia urged by Harding. It was designed to heal wounds resulting from U.S. encouragement in 1903 of Panama's independence. Colombia, without an apology, was awarded 25 million dollars.

April 21   National Farmers Union appealed to Harding for action to stabilize the nation's economy.

April 23   George Harvey, editor and Harding supporter in Chicago who had subsequently been appointed ambassador to Great Britain, published last issue of his *Harvey's Weekly.*

May 2
Supreme Court reversed the March 1920 conviction of Representative Truman H. Newberry, under federal corrupt practices act, as having spent excessive funds in the 1918 Michigan primary.

May 10
Signed executive order making 13,000 postmaster positions subject to Presidential appointment.

May 19
Signed nation's first restrictive immigration act establishing quotas for various nationalities.

Chief Justice Edward Douglass White died.

May 20
Presented $100,000 radium capsule, a gift of American women, to Mme. Curie.

May 21
Congress supported amendment by Senator William E. Borah of Idaho for an international disarmament conference.

Signed constitutionally illegal executive order transferring large oil reserves from the Navy Department to the Interior at the urging of Secretary Fall. When he later leased the Elk Hills Reserve to oilman E. L. Doheny and the Teapot Dome Reserve to H. F. Sinclair, Fall was convicted in 1929 of accepting a $100,000 bribe from Doheny in the transaction.

May 27
Signed Emergency Tariff Bill as a means to protect American farmers.

June 5
Merchant Marine Act passed to help U.S. shipping companies. Albert D. Lasker headed Shipping Board.

June 10
Signed Budget and Accounting Act establishing the Bureau of the Budget and the Office of Comptroller General.

June 23
Brigadier General Charles G. Dawes took office as Director of the Budget.

June 27
Appointed John R. McCarl as first United States Comptroller General, effective July 1.

June 30	Appointed ex-President William Howard Taft to succeed Edward Douglass White as Chief Justice. White had died on May 19.
July 1	Appointed General John Pershing as Chief of Staff.
July 2	Signed joint resolution of Congress declaring an end of a state of war with Germany.
July 11	Harding's invitation to Great Britain to attend a naval disarmament conference was made public, the day before the enabling law was signed.
July 12	Signed Naval Appropriations Bill containing clause calling for disarmament conference. Pleaded before Senate for rejection of soldiers' bonus bill. A year passed before an adjusted compensation bill was enacted.
August 9	Signed bill establishing Veterans Bureau. Colonel Charles R. Forbes named to head the bureau (he was later succeeded by General Frank T. Hines).
August 12	President's father married Alice Severns, his third wife.
August	Unemployment hit a postwar peak of 5.7 million.
August 15	Signed Packers and Stockyards Act giving Department of Agriculture authority over the meat industry.
August 24	Signed Future Trading Act limiting speculation in wheat.
	Signed amendment giving War Finance Corporation stronger role to stimulate exports of farm goods.
	Treaty of peace with Austria signed at Vienna.
August 25	Peace treaty with Germany signed in Berlin.
August 29	Peace treaty with Hungary signed at Budapest.
September 26	Addressed unofficial conference on unemployment.
October 26	Spoke in Birmingham, Alabama, on racial equality, express-

ing view that Negroes are entitled to political equality but not necessarily social and racial equality.

November 9 Signed Federal Highway Act providing federal funds for roadbuilding.

November 11 Dedicated Tomb of Unknown Soldier at Arlington Cemetery.

Ratifications of peace treaty exchanged in Berlin, final step in the procedure.

November 12 Washington Disarmament Conference opened. Delegates from England, France, Italy, Japan and the United States attended.

November 14 Proclaimed treaty with Germany. The Austrian treaty was proclaimed on November 17 and the Hungarian treaty on December 20.

November 23 Special session of 67th Congress ended.

Signed Revenue Act of 1921 reducing taxes.

Signed Sheppard-Towner Act to promote study of child hygiene and maternity welfare.

December 6 Sent annual message to Congress ending with an optimistic reference to the results of the disarmament conference.

December 13 Agreement on four-power pact reached at disarmament talks.

December 23 Commuted sentences of Debs and 23 other radicals imprisoned under wartime Espionage Act. They were released on Christmas Day.

1922

January 12 Senate voted that Representative Newberry take seat he won in 1918 election.

January New England textile workers struck in protest against lowered wages. They won a six-month strike.

January 23 Five-day conference on postwar agricultural problems started under leadership of Secretary Wallace.

February 6   Addressed closing session of naval conference. Resulting treaties limited sea power of the United States, England and Japan to a 5-5-3 ratio respectively, and guaranteed territorial integrity of China.

February 9   Signed bill establishing World War Foreign Debt Commission.

February 27   Supreme Court declared 19th Amendment constitutional.

March 4   Hubert Work of Colorado succeeded Hays as Postmaster General. Latter had resigned to become motion picture "czar."

March 20   Signed act to provide 1.5 million dollars for seed grain for farmers in crop-failure areas of the country.

March 29   Signed five-power naval armaments treaty.

April 1   Coal strike began.

April 6   Attended ceremonies establishing memorial in Arlington Cemetery honoring explorer Robert E. Peary.

April 7   Fall leased Teapot Dome oil reserve to Sinclair. Revelations then followed that he had secretly leased three of the nation's major oil reserves, including Teapot Dome.

April 15   Senator John B. Kendrick of Wyoming called in Senate for explanation of leasing.

April 29   Senate adopted resolution presented by Robert LaFollette for investigation of oil leases. Hearings of the Public Lands Committee beginning in late 1923 under Senator Thomas J. Walsh led to Fall's conviction.

May 26   Signed bill establishing Federal Narcotics Control Board.

June 14   Dedicated Francis Scott Key Memorial in Baltimore. This marked first radio broadcast by an American President.

June 21   Twenty strikebreakers killed by armed miners at Herrin, Illinois.

July 1   Strike of railroad shopmen idled trains.

July   Ordered mines reopened after conference in White House on strike.

July 14   Wrote to Fall stating his confidence in the Secretary's integrity.

August 18   Addressed Congress promising strong governmental action to end coal strike.

September 1   Federal Judge James H. Wilkerson, a Harding appointee, issued a sweeping injunction at request of Attorney General Daugherty that broke the railroad shopmen's strike.

September 5   Appointed George Sutherland of Utah to Supreme Court.

September 19   Vetoed bonus bill. Harding recognized the country's debt to veterans but saw stronger need for a balanced budget. House voted to override the veto, but the Senate backed Harding.

September 21   Signed Fordney-McCumber Act establishing record high tariffs.

Signed joint congressional resolution favoring establishment in Palestine of a national home for the Jewish people.

September 22   Signed Cable Act by which women would retain citizenship even if they married aliens.

Signed act authorizing Coal Commission to study industry problems.

November 7   In national elections, Republicans lost 70 House seats and 7 Senate seats but retained majorities in both houses.

November 20   Special session of Congress, called by Harding in hopes of getting legislature subsidizing the merchant marine, opened.

November 22   Halted sales of surplus goods at Veterans Bureau warehouse at Perryville, Maryland, outside Washington. Harding's friend and personal physician, Charles E. Sawyer, had reported to him indications of graft. However, Harding the following month raised the embargo, saying the claims of graft were "an abominable libel."

November 29 House passed the merchant marine bill. A Senate filibuster lasting into February defeated the bill.

December 4 The special session of Congress ended, and the regular session began.

December 8 Annual message sent to Congress.

December 11 Approved retirement of Mahlon Pitney, associate justice of the Supreme Court.

December 21 Pierce Butler of Minnesota appointed to Supreme Court.

1923

January 2 Accepted resignation of Fall.

January Charles R. Forbes, director of the Veterans Bureau, went to Europe, leaving his resignation effective in February. Harding was ill with influenza. About this time he saw Nan Britton for the last time.

January 29 Appointed Edward T. Sanford of Tennessee to the Supreme Court.

February 1 Charles F. Cramer, Veterans Bureau counsel and friend of Harding, resigned. A reorganization of the bureau was announced.

February 7 Personally addressed Senate to gain support for agreement negotiated with Great Britain by the Foreign Debt Commission. The terms were approved by Congress.

February 12 Senate ordered an investigation of the Veterans Bureau scandal.

February 15 Forbes resigned.

February 24 Sought Senate consent for the United States to join World Court.

February 27   Named Harry Stewart New of Indiana to' succeed Hubert Work as Postmaster General.

February 28   Signed amendment settling terms of war indebtedness by Great Britain to the United States.

March 4   Hubert Work became Secretary of Interior.

Fall retired to his New Mexico ranch.

Congressional session ended.

Harding signed law giving the Secretary of the Interior jurisdiction to determine claims to oil rights in the Red River area between Texas and Oklahoma.

March 5   Harry New took office as Postmaster General.

Harding left for vacation on houseboat of his friend, Ned McLean.

March 14   With Senate investigation due in Veterans Bureau scandal, Cramer's body was found in his Washington home in the morning. He apparently had killed himself with a gun. Harding would not accept from the FBI a letter addressed to him by Cramer. It was subsequently destroyed unopened by the Department of Justice. Forbes was later imprisoned for graft in connection with the bureau.

March 17   Daugherty stated publicly that Harding would seek a second term. The announcement embarrassed Harding, and Daugherty admitted it was unauthorized.

April 9   The Supreme Court ruled unconstitutional a minimum wage law for women and children.

April 24   At an Associated Press luncheon, Harding clarified his position urging United States participation in the World Court. He reiterated his opposition to the League of Nations and denied that participation in the court was a move toward League membership.

May 4   New York State Assembly repealed the state's prohibition enforcement act. Governor Alfred E. Smith signed the repeal, despite Harding warning that federal authorities would enforce the Volstead Act if the states did not.

May 30 Jess W. Smith, Ohioan "fixer" and White House favorite with Daugherty, killed himself with a gun after he lost favor with Harding. It was rumored he had been murdered because of all he knew about graft practices in the Harding administration.

June Sold Marion *Star* for $550,000.

June 20 Embarked on extensive "voyage of understanding" to the West, Canada and Alaska intended to restore faith in his administration. He was accompanied by 65 persons, including Cabinet members Wallace, Hoover and Work. On the tour he made 85 public speeches. Initial speeches included St. Louis (on World Court), Hutchinson, Kansas (on farm aid), and Denver (to veterans).

June 21 Nan Britton sailed on vacation trip to Europe.

June 29 Spoke in Helena, Montana, and reassured labor that his administration was friendly to it.

July 4 Sailed from Tacoma for Alaska on Navy transport *Henderson*. Traveled three weeks there, including a July 8 stop at Metlakahtla.

July 26 Gave a speech of fellowship at Vancouver, B.C., to a "good neighbor," Canada.

July 27 Reviewed fleet in Puget Sound. Spoke in Seattle although he was ill.

July 28 At Grant's Pass, Oregon, his illness was diagnosed as ptomaine. His California plans, including a speech slated for July 31 in San Francisco, were cancelled.

August 2 Died at 7:35 p.m. in San Francisco hotel. His age was 58. A final medical report gave apoplexy as the cause of death.

AFTERMATH

August 3 Coolidge sworn in as President by his own father in Plymouth, Vermont.

August 7   Harding's body reached Washington, D.C., after transcontinental train trip.

August 10   Body buried in Marion.

October   Public hearings opened on oil scandals by Senate committee headed by Thomas J. Walsh.

1924

February 8   Joint resolution of Congress ordered that oil leases be annulled and canceled.

March 28   Attorney General Daugherty resigned at the request of President Coolidge.

1927

March 4   Daugherty acquitted after being tried for conspiracy.

1929

October 25   Former Secretary of the Interior Albert B. Fall found guilty of accepting a bribe and sentenced to a year in prison and a fine of $100,000.

1931

June 16   Dedication of a memorial to Harding at Marion, after embarrassing delays. President Hoover said:

> "Warren Harding had a dim realization that he had been betrayed ·by a few of the men he had trusted, by men he believed were his devoted friends. It was later proved in the courts of the land that these men had betrayed not only the friendship of their stanch and loyal friend but they had betrayed their country. That was the tragedy of the life of Warren Harding."

ON THE LEAGUE OF NATIONS
August 28, 1920

In this "front porch" speech delivered in Marion, the Republican presidential candidate reiterated his opposition to American participation in the League of Nations and outlined his views on means of international cooperation.

Ladies and Gentlemen of the Indiana delegation:

I greet you in a spirit of rejoicing; not a rejoicing in the narrow personal or partisan sense, not in the gratifying prospects of party triumph; not in the contemplation of abundance in the harvest fields and ripening corn fields and maturing orchards; not in the reassuring approach of stability after a period of wiggling and wobbling which magnified our uncertainty—though all of these are ample for our wide rejoicing—but I rejoice that America is still free and independent and in a position of self-reliance and holds to the right of self-determination, which are priceless possessions in the present turbulence of the world.

Let us suppose the senate had ratified the peace treaty containing the league covenant as submitted to it by the President in July of last year, what would be the situation confronting our common country today? To my mind there is but one answer. Before this day we would have been called upon to fulfill the obligations which we had assumed under Article 10 of the League Covenant, to preserve the territorial integrity of Poland "as against external aggression."

I shall not now attempt to measure the boundless sympathy for the just aspirations and restored independence of Poland. Our present concern is the international situation which Poland has brought to our attention.

The council of the League of Nations would have reasoned, and reasoned correctly, that the United States could furnish the munitions and, if necessary, the men to withstand the hordes advancing from Russia far more easily than could the exhausted nations of Europe. Moreover, inasmuch as this would be the first test of the scheme of world government which was formulated and demanded by the President, speaking for the United States, the fact of a special responsibility, resting upon our shoulders, manifestly would have been undeniable. Undoubtedly the League Council, in "advising upon the means" by which the obligations to Poland should be fulfilled, as provided in the Covenant, would have so held, and probably the conscience of America, certainly the opinion of the world would have sustained that judgment.

The conclusion that our country might now be confronted by such a situation, if the Senate had ratified the League Covenant, requires no stretch

17

of the imagination. None can deny that it is possible. To many candid minds, as to my own, such a distressing situation will seem highly probable. Let us assume that the ratification had taken place. Let us assume, further, that the performance of the allotted task required the waging of war upon the Russian people, as, of course, it would, what would result; what would of necessity have to result? Nothing necessarily, we are glibly informed, since only the Congress can declare war, and the Congress might reject the appeal of the executive. But would the Congress do that? Could the Congress do that without staining indelibly the honor of the nation?

I answer "No," and I say it not on my own authority alone. Back of my judgment stands the President of the United States. Upon that point there is first-hand information. In the course of the discussion which took place at the meeting of the President and the Senate Committee on Foreign Relations, I raised the question by stating a hypothetical case precisely analogous to that which I have depicted, and then inquired whether we might not rightfully be regarded as a perfidious people if we should fail to contribute an armed force, if called upon to do so. The President first replied, as I thought somewhat evasively, that we "would be our own judges as to whether we were obliged in those circumstances to act in that way not." Pressed further, however, in response to a query incorporating the assumption that "the case provided for and prescribed had arisen" and that "the extraneous attack did exist precisely as it does exist today in Poland," the President admitted specifically that "we would be untrue if we did not keep our word."

Replying further to a question which perhaps I ought not to have considered necessary, the President pronounced a moral obligation "of course, superior to a legal obligation" and of "a greater binding force."

What then becomes of the argument that Congress, not the President, in this instance, at any rate, might "keep us out of war?" Technically, of course, it could do so. Morally, with equal certainty, it could not do so nor would it ever do so. The American people would never permit a repudiation of a debt of honor. No Congress would ever dare make this nation appear as a welcher, as it would appear and would be in such an event before the eyes of the world.

Am I not right, my countrymen, in saying that we needed only the outbreak of war between Poland and Russia to make us realize at least one of the things which, in the words of Secretary Lansing, we would have been "let in for," but for the restraining hand of the Senate, and to fetch home to us the danger of committing our country in advance to causes that we know not of?

One can have no quarrel with those who have convinced themselves that our underlying purpose in entering the great conflict was to create a league of nations. The fact remains, however, that no such intent was officially acclaimed, no allusion, nor even a suggestion to that effect appeared in the joint resolution of Congress which declared the existence of a state of war between this country and Germany. For myself I left no room for doubt of the motives which led me to cast my vote in favor of that resolution. It so happened that I made the concluding speech upon the war resolution, from my place in the Senate, on the night of April 4, 1917. These were my own words at that time:

"I want it known to the people of my state and to the nation that I am voting for war tonight for the maintenance of just American rights, which is the first essential to the preservation of the soul of this Republic.

"I vote for this joint resolution to make war, not a war thrust upon us, if I could choose the language of the resolution, but a war declared in response to affronts; a war that will at least put a soul into our American life; a war not for the cause of the allies of Europe; a war not for France, beautiful as the sentiment may be in reviving at least our gratitude to the French people; not precisely a war for civilization, worthy and inspiring as that would be; but a war that speaks for the majesty of a people properly governed, who finally are brought to the crucial test where they are resolved to get together and wage a conflict for the maintenance of their rights and the preservation of the covenant inherited from their fathers.

"We have given to the world the spectacle of a great nation that could make war without selfish intent. We unsheathed the sword some eighteen years ago for the first time in the history of the world, in the name of humanity, and we gave proof to the world at that time of an unselfish nation. Now, whether it is the fate or fortune, or travail of destiny, it has come to us to unsheathe the sword again, not alone for humanity's sake—though that splendid inspiration will be involved—but to unsheathe the sword against a great power in the maintenance of the rights of the Republic, in the maintenance which will give to us a new guaranty of nationality. That's the great thing, and I want it known, Mr. President and Senators, that this is the impelling thought with me for one, when I cast my vote."

It is for that same "guaranty of nationality" that I stand today, and shall continue to stand inflexibly, so long as I shall be permitted to live . . .

But I have a special reason for making this reference today. I challenge the statement that the patriotism which holds America first comprehends either narrowness or selfishness, or implies tacit suspicion and jealousy of other peoples. On the contrary, it is the bearer of the greatest good will, the kindliest of feeling, the best of fraternity and the most helpful of spirits. . . .

To attribute meanness to those of us who, in the performance of our public duty, refused to participate in what we sincerely regarded as a betrayal of our own country in the interest of others, is to discredit the intelligence and discrimination of the great mass of American people who directly, by their votes, put us in our positions of trust. For myself, I yield to no man in willingness, aye, in eagerness, to render the greatest conceivable assistance to the stricken peoples of Europe. . . .

It was with that feeling of sympathy and desire to serve, that most reluctantly and with grave misgivings, as I announced at the time, I voted to accept the League Covenant with reservations designed to preserve our essential liberty of action. The record is made, and under the same condition, confronted by the same alternative, I should vote now as I voted then.

But the conditions have changed. Experience has brought enlightenment. We know now that the league constituted at Versailles is utterly impotent as a preventive of wars. It is so obviously impotent that it has not even been tried. It could not survive a single test. The original League, mistakenly conceived and unreasonably insisted upon, has undoubtedly passed beyond the possibility of restoration. The maturer judgment of the world will be that it deserved to pass for the very simple reason that, contrary to all of the tendencies developed by the civilizing processes of the world, it rested upon the power of might, not of right.

The assertion is made frequently that through the surrender of our nationality, we might have saved the life of the Covenant, that is to say that, although twenty-eight nations could not make it function, one added to the twenty-eight would have achieved a glowing success, provided, always, that the one were America.

This pays to America the tribute of exceptional influence, but I suggest that if the world is dependent upon our action to bring about the supreme realization, then we ought to have the say about our own freedom in participating therein. But let us consider what is meant by this reliance upon America. What can it signify if not that it is to the United States, and to the United States alone, that the other twenty-eight nations look for the bone and sinew, the money, the munitions and the men to sustain the entire organization, not as an agency of peace, but as an armed force?

A few days ago a delegation of an organization, which calls itself a Society for the Prevention of War, appealed to the premier of Great Britain to unite and use the powers of the world in defense of Poland, Armenia and the Dardanells. The British premier replied, according to his remarks quoted by the newspapers, to the effect that, while the formation of "an international army" would be "an ideal solution," it could not be accomplished because European nations could not furnish the troops, and the United States had "withdrawn from cooperation,"—a polite and diplomatic phrase and more exactly meaning, of course, that the Senate of the United States had not completed the partial obligation assumed by the President to do that very thing, that is, to "furnish the troops." Could a clearer indication of what would have been expected of this country as a member of the League be desired? Hardly. Some, too, think, or say they think, that this extraordinary service should be rendered. I do not agree with them, but, assuming that they are right, I venture to note that nothing stands in the way of performance. The President has only to call upon Congress to declare war, and to confer upon him specific authority to raise armies for the protection of the powers, which though recently associated with, are still foreign to, our own republic.

It is reasonably safe to assume, however, that the President will not pursue this course. Fortunately, he is under no "compelling moral obligation" under the League to do so. His recent unhappy experience, moreover, in asking Congress to send American boys to police Armenia would hardly encourage repetition of a request already courteously but quite firmly declined by the Congress. What then, in like circumstances, would be the answer of the British premier himself? One does not have far to seek this available advice. In his own words, addressing a meeting of the Coalition Liberals on August 12 last, according to the press reports, he said:

"When the terrible question of peace or war has to be decided, our first duty as a government is to the people, who trust us not to commit their treasure to any unjustifiable adventure. Nothing but the most imperative call of national honor, national safety and national freedom can justify war. Before this country is committed to it, even in the most limited form, we must be satisfied that these are in peril."

I quote these telling words, my countrymen, with the utmost satisfaction, because with one amendment they express to a nicety my own position. I take for granted that the prime minister meant to include in "treasure," the greatest treasure of all, but, for myself, I should leave nothing to be inferred. Foremost and above all else to be safeguarded by those of us who hold the trust of the people, it goes without saying, but can not be too often repeated, is the manhood of the nation. American boys are not born to be made the sacrifices of war, except when it is clearly and unmistakably in defense of their country.

Now, it may appear to you that I have been speaking chiefly in the negative. I make the admission. What is more, I might continue to do so almost indefinitely without disadvantage to our cause. So many things have been done by the present expiring administration that no power on earth could induce me to do, that I cannot even attempt to recount them. I may remark casually, however, that if I should be, as I fully expect to be, elected President of this just and honorable Republic, I will not empower an Assistant Secretary of the Navy to draft a constitution for helpless neighbors in the West Indies and jam it down their throats at the point of bayonets borne by United States marines. We have a higher service for our gallant marines than that. Nor will I misuse the power of the executive to cover with a veil of secrecy repeated acts of unwarranted interference in domestic affairs of the little republics of the western hemisphere, such as in the past few years have not only made enemies of those who should be our friends, but have rightfully discredited our country as their trusted neighbor.

On the other hand, I will not or shall not, as you prefer, submit to any wrong against any American citizen, with respect to either his life or his property, by any government. This statement is made in all solemnity, with enmity for none and friendship for all. If it particularly applies to Mexico, the application has been directed by the robbery and murder of hundreds of our own people in that unhappy country, who were lawfully there and were entitled to protection. One must admit that these outrages upon Americans are largely the consequences of the wiggling and wobbling, the supine waiting of our own government, though the admission neither helps the hurt, nor gives the hope of security for the future while the present administration remains in power or when one in "complete accord" succeeds it.

This admonition is not directed exclusively toward our next-door neighbor to whom we would gladly hold forth a helping hand, and whom primarily, certainly in preference to far-off peoples in Europe, Asia and Africa, it is our manifest duty to serve with a whole heart and generous tolerance. It is intended for a plain notice to every government on the face of the earth that the entire resources of this nation are pledged to maintain the sacredness of American lives and the just protection of American properties. This is not bombast, my countrymen, it is a note of assurance which is the right of American citizenship. You know that I am not given to exaggeration or undue emphasis. It is a simple fact, or rather, speaking more precisely, it is going to be the fact if you elect me President.

The line of demarcation between our attitude and that of our political opponents is perfectly plain. The President has made his position clear by his acts no less than by his words. Twice there came to him an opportunity to obtain ratification at the hands of the Senate, and twice he put the opportunity aside, because he would not accept reservations designed solely to safeguard American rights. He still holds Article 10 to be the heart of the Covenant. So does the Democratic platform. So does the Democratic nominee. To assume that the nominee would accept the reservations rejected by the President and denounced by the party platform is to impugn his integrity. To insinuate, as those who in proclaiming themselves for the Democratic candidate and "the League with reservations" do insinuate that he would pursue such a course in seeking ratification is not to pay him a compliment, but rather to challenge his sincerity.

For myself I do not question for a moment the truth of what the Democratic nominee says on this subject. He has flatly said he is "in favor of going in" on the basis announced by the President. I am not. That is the whole difference between us, but it is a most vital one, because it involves the disparity between a World Court of Justice supplemented by a World Association for conference, on the one hand, and the Council of the League on the other.

The difference between a court of international justice and the council created by the League Covenant is simple but profound.

The one is a judicial tribunal to be governed by fixed and definite principles of law administered without passion or prejudice. The other is an association of diplomats and politicians whose determinations are sure to be influenced by considerations of expediency and national selfishness. The difference is one with which Americans are familiar, the old and fundamental difference between a government of laws and a government of men.

I do not mean to say, nor do I mean to permit any such construction, that I would decline to cooperate with other nations in an honest endeavor to prevent wars. Nobody living would take that position. The only question is one of method or of practicability within the bounds prescribed by fundamental principles.

There are distinctly two types of international relationship. One is an offensive and defensive alliance of great powers, like that created at Versailles, to impose their will upon the helpless peoples of the world. Frankly, I am opposed to such a scheme as that, and I speak knowingly when I say that the associated powers, with whom we fought the war, were reluctant to accept such a proposition.

I am opposed to the very thought of our Republic becoming a party to so gross an outrage upon other peoples, who have as good a right to seek their political freedom as we had in 1776 and have the same right to developing eminence under the inspiration of nationality as we held for ourselves.

The other type is a Society of Free Nations, or an Association of Free Nations, or a League of Free Nations, animated by considerations of right and justice, instead of might and self-interest, and not merely proclaimed an agency in pursuit of peace, but so organized and so participated in as to make the actual attainment of peace a reasonable possibility. Such an association I favor with all my heart, and I would make no fine distinction as to whom credit is due. One need not care what it is called. Let it be an Association, a Society, or a League, or what not, our concern is solely with the substance, not the form thereof.

This is proposing no new thing. This country is already a member of such a society—The Hague Tribunal, which, unlike the League of Versailles, is still functioning, and within a few weeks will resume its committee sessions under the chairmanship of an American representative.

In that body we have the framework of a really effective instrumentality of enduring peace. The fact that the tribunal did not prevent the Great War is, of course, manifest, but the cause of the failure is no less apparent. Germany, already secretly determined upon a ruthless invasion, was able to prevent the adoption of measures which might have proved effectual. The condition now is wholly different. Not only Germany, but the entire world has profited to the extent of an awful object lesson, the impressions of which can not be erased from the human mind for generations to come. The horrors of war and the eagerness for peace have become universal. What once seemed at The Hague to be a mere academic discussion has become a positive, outstanding need of facing terrifying actualities. This makes vastly easier the task of so strengthening The Hague Tribunal as to render its just decrees either acceptable or enforceable. It is not uncommon for the advocates of the League of Versailles unfavorably to contrast with it the Hague Tribunal upon the ground that the Tribunal "lacks teeth."

Very well, then, let's put teeth into it. If, in the failed League of Versailles, there can be found machinery which the Tribunal can use properly and advantageously, by all means let it be appropriated. I would even go further. I would take and combine all that is good and excise all that is bad from both organizations. This statement is broad enough to include the suggestion that if the League, which has heretofore riveted our considerations and apprehensions, has been so entwined and interwoven into the peace of Europe, that its good must be preserved in order to stabilize the peace of that continent then it can be amended or revised so that we may still have a remnant of the world's aspirations of 1918 builded into the world's highest conception of helpful cooperation in the ultimate realization.

I believe humanity would welcome the creation of an international association for conference and a world court whose verdicts upon justiciable questions this country in common with all nations would be both willing and able to uphold. The decision of such a court or the recommendations of such a conference could be accepted without sacrificing on our part, or asking any other power to sacrifice, one iota of nationality.

The Democratic nominee has spoken about America abandoning her associates in war and deserting the allied nations in establishing the League of Versailles. I do not think it longer necessary to challenge that statement or pass further opinion upon the unfortunate League. It has already been abandoned by Europe, which had gone so far as to accept it by formal agreement in treaty. On this subject, we are fully informed at first hand. Only the other day the British premier said unresentfully that the essential cooperation of America might involve "some change, at any rate, in the form of the Covenant," and he added, with characteristic outspokeness, "It is quite possible it might be a change for the better." Compare this with the obstinate insistence of the President and the Democratic nominee upon acceptance of the original document with only such "interpretations" as neither safeguard our liberties nor bind other powers in the slightest degree to the recognition of our just and proper reservations.

Listen, further, to the wise and far-seeing former British ambassador, who was not permitted to present his credentials to our executive.

"As long," said Viscount Grey, hardly a month ago, "as long as the richest, most powerful, the greatest, both for population and territory, of the civilized countries of the world stands outside the League, the League will be unable to fulfill its destiny. To put it in quite plain terms, the Americans must be told that if they will only join the League they can practically name their own terms." Undoubtedly that is the fact. I ask: Is there any good reason why we should not avail ourselves of this privilege? I do not mean in any arrogant, or domineering, or patronizing, or selfish way, but simply as a matter of fairness and right to our own people. Surely it is becoming, and a duty as well, to safeguard our own people, since it is we who are the main contributors, while asking nothing for ourselves except to participate in a contribution to the promotion of world peace. Would not Great Britain, in like circumstances, exercise such a prerogative? Would not France? Would not any nation rejoicing in nationality, buttressed by common-sense?

Viscount Grey continues: "The Americans should be entrusted with the task of drafting a reconstruction scheme." Then he suggests further that "a committee of the Senate—we must never forget the Senate's rights and duties in regard to foreign affairs being reinforced by the members of the House of Representatives, and also by nominees of the President, and Supreme Court—could draw up suggestions for the reconstruction of the League, which would be consonant with the feeling not of one, but of all parties in America."

Frankly, I value that suggestion very highly, because it is proffered obviously in a helpful and friendly spirit and reveals an important Old World opinion on the necessary of amendment, revision or reconstruction. It comprehends substantially what I would propose to do if elected President. I do not mean precisely that. It would be clearly unwise to undertake specific suggestions now. What is in my mind is the wisdom of calling into real conference the ablest and most experienced minds of this country, from whatever walks of life they may be derived and without regard to party affiliation, to formulate a definite, practical plan along the lines already indicated for the consideration of the controlling foreign powers.

The objection, strongly uttered in some quarters, that this course would involve the reconvening of the entire convention may be regarded as a very slight one. The acceptance of our proposals by the few principal nations would undoubtedly be followed promptly by the acceptance on the part of the minor members of the alliance . . . .

I have already announced that I shall urge prompt passage of the resolution vetoed by the President, declaring at an end the preposterous condition of technical war when we are actually at peace. Simultaneously, I shall naturally advise the resumption by the Congress of its exceptional powers, which have been vested by war legislation in the executive. I have no expectation whatever of finding it necessary or advisable to negotiate a separate peace with Germany.

In view of the simple fact that the Allied powers with whom we were associated in the war have already formally concluded their peace, the passage of the peace resolution by Congress would merely give formal recognition to an obvious fact. . . .

Mindful of our splendid example and renewing every obligation of association in war, I want America to be the rock of security at home, resolute in righteousness and unalterable in security and supremacy of the law. Let us be done with wiggling and wobbling. Steady, America! Let us assure good fortune to all. We may maintain our eminence as a great people at home and resume our high place in the estimate of the world. Our moral leadership was lost when "Ambition" sought to superimpose a reactionary theory of discredited autocracy upon the progressive principle of living, glowing democracy. My chief aspiration, my countrymen, if clothed with power, will be to regain that lost leadership, not for myself, not even for my party, though honoring and trusting it as I do, but for my country, the country that I love from the bottom of my heart, and with every fibre of my being, above all else in the world.

INAUGURAL ADDRESS
March 4, 1921

Speaking on the Capitol's east portico, Harding broadly reviewed the action needed to bring the country back to the "normal way" after the war. His address was called by a Briton "the most illiterate statement ever made by the head of a civilized government."

My Countrymen:

When one surveys the world about him after the great storm, noting the marks of destruction and yet rejoicing in the ruggedness of the things which withstood it, if he is an American he breathes the clarified atmosphere with a strange mingling of regret and new hope. We have seen a world passion spend its fury, but we contemplate our Republic unshaken, and hold our civilization secure. Liberty—liberty within the law—and civilization are inseparable, and though both were threatened we find them now secure; and there comes to Americans the profound assurance that our representative government is the highest expression and surest guaranty of both.

Standing in this presence, mindful of the solemnity of this occasion, feeling the emotions which no one may know until he senses the great weight of responsibility for himself, I must utter my belief in the divine inspiration of the founding fathers. Surely there must have been God's intent in the making of this new-world Republic. Ours is an organic law which had but one ambiguity, and we saw that effaced in a baptism of sacrifice and blood, with union maintained, the Nation supreme, and its concord inspiring. We have seen the world rivet its hopeful gaze on the great truths on which the founders wrought. We have seen civil, human, and religious liberty verified and glorified. In the beginning the Old World scoffed at our experiment; today our foundations of political and social belief stand unshaken, a precious inheritance to ourselves, an inspiring example of freedom and civilization to all mankind. Let us express renewed and strengthened devotion, in grateful reverence for the immortal beginning, and utter our confidence in the supreme fulfillment.

The recorded progress of our Republic, materially and spiritually, in itself proves the wisdom of the inherited policy of non-involvement in Old World affairs. Confident of our ability to work out our own destiny, and jealously guarding our right to do so, we seek no part in directing the destinies of the Old World. We do not mean to be entangled. We will accept no responsibility except as our own conscience and judgment, in each instance, may determine.

Our eyes never will be blind to a developing menace, our ears never deaf to the call of civilization. We recognize the new order in the world, with the closer contacts which progress has wrought. We sense the call of the human heart for fellowship, fraternity, and co-operation. We crave friendship and harbor no hate. But America, our America, the America builded on the foundation laid by the inspired fathers, can be a party to no permanent military alliance. It can enter into no political commitments, nor assume any economic obligations which will subject our decisions to any other than our own authority.

I am sure our own people will not misunderstand, nor will the world misconstrue. We have no thought to impede the paths to closer relationship. We wish to promote understanding. We want to do our part in making offensive warfare so hateful that Governments and peoples who resort to it must prove the righteousness of their cause or stand as outlaws before the bar of civilization.

We are ready to associate ourselves with the nations of the world, great and small, for conference, for counsel; to seek the expressed views of world opinion; to recommend a way to approximate disarmament and relieve the crushing burdens of military and naval establishments. We elect to participate in suggesting plans for mediation, conciliation, and arbitration, and would gladly join in that expressed conscience of progress, which seeks to clarify and write the laws of international relationship, and establish a world court for the disposition of such justiciable questions as nations are agreed to submit thereto. In expressing aspirations, in seeking practical plans, in translating humanity's new concept of righteousness and justice and its hatred of war into recommended action we are ready most heartily to unite, but every commitment must be made in the exercise of our national sovereignty. Since freedom impelled, and independence inspired, and nationality exalted, a world super-government is contrary to everything we cherish and can have no sanction by our Republic. This is not selfishness, it is sanctity. It is no aloofness, it is security. It is not suspicion of others, it is patriotic adherence to the things which made us what we are.

Today, better than ever before, we know the aspirations of human-kind, and share them. We have come to a new realization of our place in the world and a new appraisal of our Nation by the world. The unselfishness of these United States is a thing proven; our devotion to peace for ourselves, and for the world is well established; our concern for preserved civilization has had its impassioned and heroic expression. There was no American failure to resist the attempted reversion of civilization; there will be no failure today or tomorrow.

The success of our popular government rests wholly upon the correct interpretation of the deliberate, intelligent, dependable popular will of America. In a deliberate questioning of a suggested change of national policy, where internationality was to supersede nationality, we turned to a referendum, to the American people. There was ample discussion, and there is a public mandate in manifest understanding.

America is ready to encourage, eager to initiate, anxious to participate in any seemly program likely to lessen the probability of war, and promote that brotherhood of mankind which must be God's highest conception of human relationship. Because we cherish ideals of justice and peace, because we appraise international comity and helpful relationship no less highly than any people of the world, we aspire to a high place in the moral leadership of civilization, and we hold a maintained America, the proven Republic, the unshaken temple of representative democracy, to be not only an inspiration and example, but the highest agency of strengthening good will and promoting accord on both continents.

Mankind needs a world-wide benediction of understanding. It is needed among individuals, among peoples, among governments, and it will inaugurate an era of good feeling to mark the birth of a new order. In such understanding men will strive confidently for the promotion of their better relationships and nations will promote the comities so essential to peace.

We must understand that ties of trade bind nations in closest intimacy, and none may receive except as he gives. We have not strengthened ours in accordance with our resources or our genius, notably on our own continent, where a galaxy of Republics reflects the glory of new-world democracy, but in the new order of finance and trade we mean to promote enlarged activities and seek expanded confidence.

Perhaps we can make no more helpful contribution by example than prove a Republic's capacity to emerge from the wreckage of war. While the world's embittered travail did not leave us devastated lands nor desolated cities, left no gaping wounds, no breast with hate, it did involve us in the delirium of expenditure, in expanded currency and credits, in unbalanced industry, in unspeakable waste, and disturbed relationships. While it uncovered our portion of hateful selfishness at home, it also revealed the heart of America as sound and fearless, and beating in confidence unfailing.

Amid it all we have riveted the gaze of all civilization to the unselfishness and the righteousness of representative democracy, where our freedom never has made offensive warfare, never has sought territorial aggrandizement through force, never has turned to the arbitrament of arms until reason has been exhausted. When the Governments of the earth shall have established a freedom like our own and shall have sanctioned the pursuit of peace as we have practiced it, I believe the last sorrow and the final sacrifice of international warfare will have been written.

Let me speak to the maimed and wounded soldiers who are present today, and through them convey to their comrades the gratitude of the Republic for their sacrifices in its defense. A generous country will never forget the services you rendered, and you may hope for a policy under Government that will relieve any maimed successors from taking your places on another such occasion as this.

Our supreme task is the resumption of our onward, normal way. Reconstruction, readjustment, restoration—all these must follow. I would like to hasten them. If it will lighten the spirit and add to the resolution with which we take up the task, let me repeat for our Nation, we shall give no people just cause to make war upon us; we hold no national prejudices; we entertain no spirit of revenge; we do not hate; we do not covet; we dream of no conquest, nor boast of armed prowess.

If, despite this attitude, war is again forced upon us, I earnestly hope a way may be found which will unify our individual and collective strength and consecrate all America, materially and spiritually, body and soul, to national defense. I can vision the ideal republic, where every man and woman is called under the flag for assignment to duty for whatever service, military or civic, the individual is best fitted; where we may call to universal service every plant, agency, or facility, all in the sublime sacrifice for country, and not one penny of war profit shall inure to the benefit of private individual, corporation, or combination, but all above the normal shall flow into the defense chest of the Nation. There is something inherently wrong, something out of accord with the ideals of representative democracy, when one portion of our citizenship turns its activities to private gain amid defensive war while another is fighting, sacrificing, or dying for national preservation.

Out of such universal service will come a new unity of spirit and purpose, a new confidence and consecration, which would make our defense impregnable, our triumph assured. Then we should have little or no disorganizing of our economic, industrial, and commercial systems at home, no staggering war debts, no swollen fortunes to flout the sacrifices of our soldiers, no excuse for sedition. no pitiable slackerism, no outrage of treason. Envy and jealousy would have no soil for their menacing development, and revolution would be without the passion which engenders it.

A regret for the mistakes of yesterday must not, however, blind us to the tasks of today. War never left such an aftermath. There has been staggering loss of life and measureless wastage of materials. Nations are still groping for return to stable ways. Discouraging indebtedness confronts us like all the war-torn nations, and these obligations must be provided for. No civilization can survive repudiation.

We can reduce the abnormal expenditures, and we will. We can strike at war taxation, and we must. We must face the grim necessity, with full knowledge that the task is to be solved, and we must proceed with a full realization that no statute enacted by man can repeal the inexorable laws of nature. Our most dangerous tendency is to expect too much of government, and at the same time do for it too little.

We contemplate the immediate task of putting our public household in order. We need a rigid and yet sane economy, combined with fiscal justice, and it must be attended by individual prudence and thrift, which are so essential to this trying hour and reassuring for the future.

The business world reflects the disturbance of war's reaction. Herein flows the lifeblood of material existence. The economic mechanism is intricate and its parts interdependent, and has suffered the shocks and jars incident to abnormal demands, credit inflations, and price upheavals. The normal balances have been impaired, the channels of distribution have been clogged, the relations of labor and management have been strained. We must seek the readjustment with care and courage. Our people must give and take. Prices must reflect the receding fever of war activities. Perhaps we never shall know the old levels of wages again, because war invariably readjusts compensations, and the necessaries of life will show their inseparable relationship, but we must strive for normalcy to reach stability. All the penalities will not be light, nor evenly distributed. There is no way of making them so. There is no instant step from disorder to order. We must face a condition of grim reality, charge off our losses and start afresh. It is the oldest lesson of civilization. I would like government to do all it can to mitigate; then, in understanding, in mutuality of interest, in concern for the common good, our tasks will be solved. No altered system will work a miracle. Any wild experiment will only add to the confusion. Our best assurance lies in efficient administration of our proven system.

The forward course of the business cycle is unmistakable. Peoples are turning from destruction to production. Industry has sensed the changed order and our own people are turning to resume their normal, onward way. The call is for productive America to go on. I know that Congress and the Administration will favor every wise Government policy to aid the resumption and encourage continued progress.

I speak for administrative efficiency, for lightened tax burdens, for sound commercial practices, for adequate credit facilities, for sympathetic concern for all agricultural problems, for the omission of unnecessary interference of Government with business, for an end to Government's experiment in business, and for more efficient business in Government administration. With all of this must attend a mindfulness of the human side of all activities, so that social, industrial, and economic justice will be squared with the purposes of a righteous people.

With the nation-wide induction of womanhood into our political life, we may count upon her intuitions, her refinements, her intelligence, and her influence to exalt the social order. We count upon her exercise of the full privileges and the performance of the duties of citizenship to speed the attainment of the highest state.

I wish for an America no less alert in guarding against dangers from within than it is watchful against enemies from without. Our fundamental law recognizes no class, no group, no section; there must be none in legislation or administration. The supreme inspiration is the common weal. Hu-

manity hungers for international peace, and we crave it with all mankind.
My most reverent prayer for America is for industrial peace, with its rewards, widely and generally distributed, amid the inspirations of equal
opportunity. No one justly may deny the equality of opportunity which
made us what we are. We have mistaken unpreparedness to embrace it to
be a challenge of the reality, and due concern for making all citizens fit for
participation will give added strength of citizenship and magnify our
achievement.

If revolution insists upon overturning established order, let other peoples
make the tragic experiment. There is no place for it in America. When World
War threatened civilization we pledged our resources and our lives to its
preservation, and when revolution threatens we unfurl the flag of law and
order and renew our consecration. Ours is a constitutional freedom where
the popular will is the law supreme and minorities are sacredly protected.
Our revisions, reformations, and evolutions reflect a deliberate judgment
and an orderly progress, and we mean to cure our ills, but never destroy or
permit destruction by force.

I had rather submit our industrial controversies to the conference table
in advance than to a settlement table after conflict and suffering. The earth
is thirsting for the cup of good will, understanding is its fountain source. I
would like to acclaim an era of good feeling amid dependable prosperity
and all the blessings which attend.

It has been proved again and again that we cannot, while throwing our
markets open to the world, maintain American standards of living and
opportunity, and hold our industrial eminence in such unequal competition. There is a luring fallacy in the theory of banished barriers of trade,
but preserved American standards require our higher production costs to be
reflected in our tariffs on imports. Today, as never before, when peoples
are seeking trade restoration and expansion, we must adjust our tariffs to
the new order. We seek participation in the world's exchanges, because
therein lies our way to widened influence and the triumphs of peace. We
know full well we cannot sell where we do not buy, and we cannot sell
successfully where we do not carry. Opportunity is calling not alone for
the restoration, but for a new era in production, transportation and trade.
We shall answer it best by meeting the demand of a surpassing home
market, by promoting self-reliance in production, and by bidding enterprise, genius, and efficiency to carry our cargoes in American bottoms to
the marts of the world.

We would not have an America living within and for herself alone, but
we would have her self-reliant, independent, and ever nobler, stronger, and
richer. Believing in our higher standards, reared through constitutional
liberty and maintained opportunity, we invite the world to the same
heights. But pride in things wrought is no reflex of a completed task.

Common welfare is the goal of our national endeavor. Wealth is not inimical to welfare; it ought to be its friendliest agency. There never can be equality of rewards or possessions so long as the human plan contains varied talents and differing degrees of industry and thrift, but ours ought to be a country free from the great blotches of distressed poverty. We ought to find a way to guard against the perils and penalties of unemployment. We want an America of homes, illumined with hope and happiness, where mothers, freed from the necessity for long hours of toil beyond their own doors, may preside as befits the hearthstone of American citizenship. We want the cradle of American childhood rocked under conditions so wholesome and so hopeful that no blight may touch it in its development, and we want to provide that no selfish interest, no material necessity, no lack of opportunity shall prevent the gaining of that education so essential to best citizenship.

There is no short cut to the making of these ideals into glad realities. The world has witnessed again and again the futility and the mischief of ill-considered remedies for social and economic disorders. But we are mindful today as never before of the friction of modern industrialism, and we must learn its causes and reduce its evil consequences by sober and tested methods. Where genius has made for great possibilities, justice and happiness must be reflected in a greater common welfare.

Service is the supreme commitment of life. I would rejoice to acclaim the era of the Golden Rule and crown it with the autocracy of service. I pledge an administration wherein all the agencies of Government are called to serve, and ever promote an understanding of Government purely as an expression of the popular will.

One cannot stand in this presence and be unmindful of the tremendous responsibility. The world upheaval has added heavily to our tasks. But with the realization comes the surge of high resolve, and there is reassurance in belief in the God-given destiny of our Republic. If I felt that there is to be sole responsibility in the Executive for the America of tomorrow I should shrink from the burden. But here are a hundred millions, with common concern and shared responsibility, answerable to God and country. The Republic summons them to their duty, and I invite co-operation.

I accept my part with single-mindedness of purpose and humility of spirit, and implore the favor and guidance of God in His Heaven. With these I am unafraid, and confidently face the future.

I have taken the solemn oath of office on that passage of Holy Writ wherein it is asked: "What doth the Lord require of thee but to do justly, and to love mercy, and to walk humbly with thy God?" This I plight to God and country.

ON NATIONAL PROBLEMS
April 12, 1921

*Addressing the both Houses of Congress which he had summoned
into a special session, the new President enumerated the steps
he felt were needed to get the country back to normalcy. He urged
that Congress quickly declare an end to the technical state of war
then in effect with Germany and its allies.*

Mr. Speaker, Vice President, and Members of the Congress, you have
been called in extraordinary session to give your consideration to national
problems far too pressing to be long neglected. We face our tasks of legislation and administration amid conditions as difficult as our Government has
ever contemplated. Under our political system the people of the United
States have charged the new Congress and the new administration with the
solution—the readjustments, reconstruction, and restoration which must
follow in the wake of war.

It may be regretted that we were so illy prepared for war's aftermath, so
little made ready to return to the ways of peace, but we are not to be discouraged. Indeed, we must be the more firmly resolved to undertake our
work with high hope, and invite every factor in our citizenship to join in the
effort to find our normal, onward way again.

The American people have appraised the situation, and with that tolerance and patience which go with understanding they will give to us the
influence of deliberate public opinion which ultimately becomes the edict
of any popular government. They are measuring some of the stern necessities, and will join in the give and take which is so essential to firm
reestablishment.

First in mind must be the solution of our problems at home, even though
some phases of them are inseparably linked with our foreign relations.
The surest procedure in every government is to put its own house in order.

I know of no more pressing problem at home than to restrict our national
expenditures within the limits of our national income and at the same time
measurably lift the burdens of war taxation from the shoulders of the
American people.

One can not be unmindful that economy is a much-employed cry, most
frequently stressed in preelection appeals, but it is ours to make it an outstanding and ever-impelling purpose in both legislation and administration.
The unrestrained tendency to heedless expenditure and the attending growth
of public indebtedness, extending from Federal authority to that of State
and municipality and including the smallest political subdivision, constitute
the most dangerous phase of government to-day. The Nation can not

restrain except in its own activities, but it can be exemplar in a wholesale reversal.

The staggering load of war debt must be cared for in orderly funding and gradual liquidation. We shall hasten the solution and aid effectively in lifting the tax burdens if we strike resolutely at expenditure. It is far more easily said than done. In the fever of war our expenditures were so little questioned, the emergency was so impelling, appropriation was so unimpeded that we little noted millions and counted the Treasury inexhaustible. It will strengthen our resolution if we ever keep in mind that a continuation of such a course means inevitable disaster.

Our current expenditures are running at the rate of approximately five billions a year, and the burden is unbearable. There are two agencies to be employed in correction: One is rigid resistance in appropriation and the other is the utmost economy in administration. Let us have both. I have already charged department heads with this necessity. I am sure Congress will agree; and both Congress and the administration may safely count on the support of all right-minded citizens, because the burden is theirs. The pressure for expenditure swelling the flow in one locality while draining another, is sure to defeat the imposition of just burdens, and the effect of our citizenship protesting outlay will be wholesome and helpful. I wish it might find its reflex in economy and thrift among the people themselves, because therein lies quicker recovery and added security for the future.

The estimates of receipts and expenditures and the statements as to the condition of the Treasury which the Secretary of the Treasury is prepared to present to you will indicate what revenues must be provided in order to carry on the Government's business and meet its current requirements and fixed-debt charges. Unless there are striking cuts in the important fields of expenditure, receipts from internal taxes can not safely be permitted to fall below $4,000,000,000 in the fiscal years 1922 and 1923. This would mean total internal tax collections of about one billion less than in 1920 and one-half billion less than in 1921.

The most substantial relief from the tax burden must come for the present from the readjustment of internal taxes, and the revision or repeal of those taxes which have become unproductive and are so artificial and burdensome as to defeat their own purpose. A prompt and thoroughgoing revision of the internal tax laws, made with due regard to the protection of the revenues, is, in my judgment, a requisite to the revival of business activity in this country. It is earnestly hoped, therefore, that the Congress will be able to enact without delay a revision of the revenue laws and such emergency tariff measures as are necessary to protect American trade and industry.

It is of less concern whether internal taxation or tariff revision shall come first than has been popularly imagined, because we must do both, but the practical course for earliest accomplishment will readily suggest itself to the Congress. We are committeed to the repeal of the excess-profits tax and the abolition of inequities and unjustifiable exasperations in the present system.

The country does not expect and will not approve a shifting of burdens. It is more interested in wiping out the necessity for imposing them and eliminating confusion and cost in the collection.

The urgency for an instant tariff enactment, emergency in character and understood by our people that it is for the emergency only, can not be too much emphasized. I believe in the protection of American industry, and it is our purpose to prosper America first. The privileges of the American market to the foreign producer are offered too cheaply to-day, and the effect on much of our own productivity is the destruction of our self-reliance, which is the foundation of the independence and good fortune of our people. Moreover, imports should pay their fair share of our cost of government.

One who values American prosperity and maintained American standards of wage and living can have no sympathy with the proposal that easy entry and the flood of imports will cheapen our costs of living. It is more likely to destroy our capacity to buy. To-day American agriculture is menaced, and its products are down to prewar normals, yet we are endangering our fundamental industry through the high cost of transportation from farm to market and through the influx of foreign farm products, because we offer, essentially unprotected, the best market in the world. It would be better to err in protecting our basic food industry than paralyze our farm activities in the world struggle for restored exchanges.

The maturer revision of our tariff laws should be based on the policy of protection, resisting that selfishness which turns to greed, but ever concerned with that productivity at home which is the source of all abiding good fortune. It is agreed that we can not sell unless we buy, but ability to sell is based on home development and the fostering of home markets. There is little sentiment in the trade of the world. Trade can and ought to be honorable, but it knows no sympathy. While the delegates of the nations at war were debating peace terms at Paris, and while we later debated our part in completing the peace, commercial agents of other nations were opening their lines and establishing their outposts, with a forward look to the morrow's trade. It was wholly proper, and has been advantageous to them. Tardy as we are, it will be safer to hold our own markets secure, and build thereon for our trade with the world.

A very important matter is the establishment of the Government's business on a business basis. There was toleration of the easy-going, unsystematic method of handling our fiscal affairs, when indirect taxation held the public unmindful of the Federal burden. But there is knowledge of the high cost of government to-day, and high cost of living is inseparably linked with high cost of government. There can be no complete correction of the high living cost until government's cost is notably reduced.

Let me most heartily commend the enactment of legislation providing for the national budget system. Congress has already recorded its belief in the budget. It will be a very great satisfaction to know of its early enactment, so that it may be employed in establishing the economies and business methods so essential to the minimum of expenditure.

I have said to the people we meant to have less of government in business as well as more business in government. It is well to have it understood that business has a right to pursue its normal, legitimate, and righteous way unimpeded, and it ought have no call to meet Government competition where all risk is borne by the Public Treasury. There is no challenge to honest and lawful business success. But Government approval of fortunate, untrammeled business does not mean toleration of restraint of trade or of maintained prices by unnatural methods. It is well to have legitimate business understand that a just Government, mindful of the interests of all the people, has a right to expect the cooperation of that legitimate business in stamping out the practices which add to unrest and inspire restrictive legislation. Anxious as we are to restore the onward flow of business, it is fair to combine assurance and warning in one utterance.

One condition in the business world may well receive your inquiry. Deflation has been in progress but has failed to reach the mark where it can be proclaimed to the great mass of consumers. Reduced cost of basic production has been recorded, but high cost of living has not yielded in like proportion. For example, the prices on grains and live stock has been deflated, but the cost of bread and meats is not adequately reflected therein. It is to be expected that nonperishable staples will be slow in yielding to lowered prices, but the maintained retail costs in perishable foods cannot be justified.

I have asked the Federal Trade Commission for a report of its observations, and it attributes, in the main, the failure to adjust consumers' cost to basic production costs to the exchange of information by "open-price associations," which operate, evidently, within the law, to the very great advantage of their members and equal disadvantage to the consuming public. Without the spirit of hostility or haste in accusation of profiteering, some suitable inquiry by Congress might speed the price readjustment to normal relationship, with helpfulness to both producer and consumer. A measuring rod of fair prices will satisfy the country and give us a business revival to end all depression and unemployment.

The great interest of both the producer and consumer—indeed, all our industrial and commercial life, from agriculture to finance—in the problems of transportation will find its reflex in your concern to aid reestablishment, to restore efficiency, and bring transportation cost into a helpful relationship rather than continue it as a hindrance to resumed activities.

It is little to be wondered that ill-considered legislation, the war strain, Government operation in heedlessness of cost, and the conflicting programs, or the lack of them, for restoration have brought about a most difficult situation, made doubly difficult by the low tide of business. All are so intimately related that no improvement will be permanent until the railways are operated efficiently at a cost within that which the traffic can bear.

If we can have it understood that Congress has no sanction for Government ownership, that Congress does not levy taxes upon the people to cover deficits in a service which should be self-sustaining, there will be an avowed foundation on which to rebuild.

Freight-carrying charges have mounted higher and higher until commerce is halted and production discouraged. Railway rates and costs of operation must be reduced.

Congress may well investigate and let the public understand wherein our system and the Federal regulations are lacking in helpfulness or hindering in restrictions. The remaining obstacles which are the heritage of capitalistic exploitation must be removed, and labor must join management in understanding that the public which pays is the public to be served, and simple justice is the right and will continue to be the right of all the people.

Transportation over the highways is little less important, but the problems relate to construction and development, and deserve your most earnest attention, because we are laying a foundation for a long time to come, and the creation is very difficult to visualize in its great possibilities.

The highways are not only feeders to the railroads and afford relief from their local burdens, they are actually lines of motor traffic in interstate commerce. They are the smaller arteries of the larger portion of our commerce, and the motor car has become an indispensable instrument in our political, social, and industrial life.

There is begun a new era in highway construction, the outlay for which runs far into hundreds of millions of dollars. Bond issues by road districts, counties, and States mount to enormous figures, and the country is facing such an outlay that it is vital that every effort shall be directed against wasted effort and unjustifiable expenditure.

The Federal Government can place no inhibition on the expenditure in the several States; but, since Congress has embarked upon a policy of assisting the States in highway improvement, wisely, I believe, it can assert a wholly becoming influence in shaping policy.

With the principle of Federal participation acceptably established, probably never to be abandoned, it is important to exert Federal influence in developing comprehensive plans looking to the promotion of commerce, and apply our expenditures in the surest way to guarantee a public return for money expended.

Large Federal outlay demands a Federal voice in the program of expenditure. Congress cannot justify a mere gift from the Federal purse to the several States, to be prorated among counties for road betterment. Such a course will invite abuses which it were better to guard against in the beginning.

The laws governing Federal aid should be amended and strengthened. The Federal agency of administration should be elevated to the importance and vested with authority comparable to the work before it. And Congress ought to prescribe conditions to Federal appropriations which will necessitate a consistent program of uniformity which will justify the Federal outlay.

I know of nothing more shocking than the millions of public funds wasted in improved highways, wasted because there is no policy of maintenance. The neglect is not universal, but it is very near it. There is nothing the Congress can do more effectively to end this shocking waste than condition all Federal aid on provisions for maintenance. Highways, no matter how generous the outlay for construction, cannot be maintained without patrol and constant repair. Such conditions insisted upon in the grant of Federal aid will safeguard the public which pays and guard the Federal Government against political abuses which tend to defeat the very purposes for which we authorize Federal expenditure.

Linked with rail and highway is the problem of water transportation— inland, coastwise, and transoceanic. It is not possible, on this occasion, to suggest to Congress the additional legislation needful to meet the aspirations of our people for a merchant marine. In the emergency of war we have constructed a tonnage equaling our largest expectations. Its war cost must be discounted to the actual values of peace and the large difference charged to the war emergency; and the pressing task is to turn our assets in tonnage to an agency of commerce.

It is not necessary to say it to Congress, but I have thought this to be a befitting occasion to give notice that the United States means to establish and maintain a great merchant marine.

Our differences of opinion as to a policy of upbuilding have been removed by the outstanding fact of our having builded. If the intelligent and efficient administration under the existing laws makes established service impossible, the Executive will promptly report to you. Manifestly, if our laws governing American activities on the seas are such as to give advantage to those who compete with us for the carrying of our own cargoes and those which should naturally come in American bottoms through trade exchanges, then the spirit of American fair play will assert itself to give American carriers their equality of opportunity. This Republic can never realize its righteous aspirations in commerce, can never be worthy the traditions of the early days of the expanding Republic until the millions of tons of shipping which we now possess are coordinated with our inland transportation and our shipping has

Government encouragement, not Government operation, in carrying our cargoes under our flag, over regularly operated routes, to every market in the world agreeable to American exchanges. It will strengthen American genius and management to have it understood that ours is an abiding determination, because carrying is second only to production in establishing and maintaining the flow of commerce to which we rightfully aspire.

It is proper to invite your attention to the importance of the question of radio communication and cables. To meet strategic, commercial, and political needs active encouragement should be given to the extension of American owned and operated cable and radio services. Between the United States and its possessions there should be ample communication facilities providing direct services at reasonable rates. Between the United States and other countries not only should there be adequate facilities, but these should be, so far as practicable, direct and free from foreign intermediation. Friendly cooperation should be extended to international efforts aimed at encouraging improvement of international communication facilities and designed to further the exchange of messages. Private monopolies tending to prevent the development of needed facilities should be prohibited. Government-owned facilities, wherever possible without unduly interfering with private enterprise or Government needs, should be made available for general uses. Particularly desirable is the provision of ample cable and radio services at reasonable rates for the transmission of press matter, so that the American reader may receive a wide range of news and the foreign reader receive full accounts of American activities. The daily press of all countries may well be put in position to contribute to international understandings by the publication of interesting foreign news.

Practical experience demonstrates the need for effective regulation of both domestic and international radio operation if this newer means of intercommunication is to be fully utilized. Especially needful is the provision of ample radio facilities for those services where radio only can be used, such as communication with ships at sea, with aircraft, and with out-of-the-way places. International communication by cable and radio requires cooperation between the powers concerned. Whatever the degree of control deemed advisable within the United States, Government licensing of cable landings and of radio stations transmitting and receiving international traffic seems necessary for the protection of American interests and for the securing of satisfactory reciprocal privileges.

Aviation is inseparable from either the Army or the Navy, and the Government must, in the interests of national defense, encourage its development for military and civil purposes. The encouragement of the civil development of aeronautics is especially desirable as relieving the Government largely of the expense of development, and of maintenance of an industry, now almost entirely borne by the Government through appropriations for the military, naval, and postal air services. The Air Mail Service is an important initial step in the direction of commercial aviation.

It has become a pressing duty of the Federal Government to provide for the regulation of air navigation; otherwise independent and conflicting legislation will be enacted by the various States which will hamper the development of aviation. The National Advisory Committee for Aeronautics, in a special report on this subject, has recommended the establishment of a bureau of aeronautics in the Department of Commerce for the Federal regulation of air navigation, which recommendation ought to have legislative approval.

I recommend the enactment of legislation establishing a bureau of aeronautics in the Navy Department to centralize the control of naval activities in aeronautics, and removing the restrictions on the personnel detailed to aviation in the Navy.

The Army Air Service should be continued as a coordinate combatant of the Army, and its existing organization utilized in cooperation with other agencies of the Government in the establishment of national transcontinental airways, and in cooperation with the States in the establishment of local airdromes and landing fields.

The American people expect Congress unfailingly to voice the gratitude of the Republic in a generous and practical way to its defenders in the World War, who need the supporting arm of the Government. Our very immediate concern is for the crippled soldiers and those deeply needing the helping hand of Government. Conscious of the generous intent of Congress, and the public concern for the crippled and dependent, I invited the services of a volunteer committee to inquire into the administration of the Bureau of War Risk Insurance, the Federal Board for Vocational Training, and other agencies of Government in caring for the ex-soldiers, sailors, and marines of the World War. This committee promptly reported the chief difficulty to be the imperfect organization of governmental effort, the same lack of coordination which hinders Government efficiency in many undertakings, less noticed because the need for prompt service is less appealing.

This committee has recommended, and I convey the recommendations to you with cordial approval, that all Government agencies looking to the welfare of the ex-service men should be placed under one directing head, so that the welfare of these disabled saviors of our civilization and freedom may have the most efficient direction. It may be well to make such an official the Director General of Service to War Veterans, and place under his direction all hospitalization, vocational training, war insurance, rehabilitation, and all pensions.

The immediate extension and utilization of the Government's hospital facilities in Army and Navy will bring relief to the acute conditions most complained of, and the hospital building program may be worked out to meet the needs likely to be urgent at the time of possible completion.

The whole program requires the most thoughtful attention of Congress, for we are embarking on the performance of a sacred obligation which involves the expenditure of billions in the half century before us. Congress must perfect the policy of generous gratitude, and conscientious administration must stamp out abuses in the very beginning. We must strengthen rather than weaken the moral fiber of the beneficiaries, and humanize all efforts so that rehabilitation shall be attended by respiritualization.

During the recent political canvass the proposal was made that a department of public welfare should be created. It was indorsed and commended so strongly that I venture to call it to your attention and to suggest favorable legislative consideration.

Government's obligation affirmatively to encourage development of the highest and most efficient type of citizenship is modernly accepted, almost universally. Government rests upon the body of citizenship; it cannot maintain itself on a level that keeps it out of touch and understanding with the community it serves. Enlightened governments everywhere recognize this and are giving their recognition effect in policies and programs. Certainly no government is more desirous than our own to reflect the human attitude, the purpose of making better citizens—physically, intellectually, spiritually. To this end I am convinced that such a department in the Government would be of real value. It could be made to crystallize much of rather vague generalization about social justice into solid accomplishment. Events of recent years have profoundly impressed thinking people with the need to recognize new social forces and evolutions, to equip our citizens for dealing rightly with problems of life and social order.

In the realms of education, public health, sanitation, conditions of workers in industry, child welfare, proper amusement and recreation, the elimination of social vice, and many other subjects, the Government has already undertaken a considerable range of activities. I assume the maternity bill, already strongly approved, will be enacted promptly, thus adding to our manifestation of human interest. But these undertakings have been scattered through many departments and bureaus without coordination and with much overlapping of functions which fritters energies and magnifies the cost. Many subjects of the greatest importance are handled by bureaus within Government departments which logically have no apparent relation to them. Other subjects which might well have the earnest consideration of Federal authority have been neglected or inadequately provided for. To bring these various activities together in a single department, where the whole field could be surveyed, and where their interrelationships could be properly appraised, would make for increased effectiveness, economy, and intelligence of direction. In creating such a department it should be made plain that there is no purpose to invade fields which the States have occupied. In respect of education, for example, control and administration have rested with the States, yet the Federal Government has always aided them. National appropriations in aid of educational purposes the last fiscal year were no less than $65,000,000. There need be no fear of undue centralization or of creating a Federal bureaucracy to dominate affairs better to be left in State control. We must, of course, avoid overlapping the activities by the several States, and we must ever resist the growing demand on the Federal Treasury for the performance of service for which the State is obligated to its citizenship.

Somewhat related to the foregoing human problems is the race question. Congress ought to wipe the stain of barbaric lynching from the banners of a free and orderly, representative democracy. We face the fact that many millions of people of African descent are numbered among our population, and that in a number of States they constitute a very large proportion of the total population. It is unnecessary to recount the difficulties incident to this condition, nor to emphasize the fact that it is a condition which cannot be removed. There has been suggestion, however, that some of its difficulties might be ameliorated by a humane and enlightened consideration of it, a study of its many aspects, and an effort to formulate, if not a policy, at least a national attitude of mind calculated to bring about the most satisfactory possible adjustment of relations between the races, and of each race to the national life. One proposal is the creation of a commission embracing representatives of both races, to study and report on the entire subject. The proposal has real merit. I am convinced that in mutual tolerance, understanding, charity, recognition of the interdependence of the races, and the maintenance of the rights of citizenship lies the road to righteous adjustment.

It is needless to call your attention to the unfinished business inherited from the preceding Congress. The appropriation bills for Army and Navy will have your early consideration.

Neither branch of the Government can be unmindful of the call for reduced expenditure for these departments of our national defense. The Government is in accord with the wish to eliminate the burdens of heavy armament. The United States ever will be in harmony with such a movement toward the higher attainments of peace. But we shall not entirely discard our agencies for defense until there is removed the need to defend. We are ready to cooperate with other nations to approximate disarmament, but merest prudence forbids that we disarm alone.

The naval program which had its beginning in what seemed the highest assurances of peace can carry no threat after the latest proof of our national unselfishness. The reasonable limitation of personnel may be combined with economies of administration to lift the burdens of excessive outlay.

The War Department is reducing the personnel of the Army from the maximum provided by law in June, 1920, to the minimum directed by

Congress in a subsequent enactment. When further reduction is compatible with national security, it may well have the sanction of Congress, so that a system of voluntary military training may offer to our young manhood the advantages of physical development, discipline, and commitment to service, and constitute the Army reserve in return for the training.

Nearly two and a half years ago the World War came to an end, and yet we find ourselves today in the technical state of war, though actually at peace, while Europe is at technical peace, far from tranquillity and little progressed toward the hoped-for restoration.

It ill becomes us to express impatience that the European belligerents are not yet in full agreement, when we ourselves have been unable to bring constituted authority into accord in our own relations to the formally proclaimed peace.

Little avails in reciting the causes of delay in Europe or our own failure to agree. But there is no longer excuse for uncertainties respecting some phases of our foreign relationship. In the existing League of Nations, world-governing with its super-powers, this Republic will have no part. There can be no misinterpretation, and there will be no betrayal of the deliberate expression of the American people in the recent election; and, settled in our decision for ourselves, it is only fair to say to the world in general, and to our associates in war in particular, that the League covenant can have no sanction by us.

The aim to associate nations to prevent war, preserve peace, and promote civilization our people most cordially applauded. We yearned for this new instrument of justice, but we can have no part in a committal to an agency of force in unknown contingencies; we can recognize no superauthority.

Manifestly the highest purpose of the League of Nations was defeated in linking it with the treaty of peace and making it the enforcing agency of the victors of the war. International association for permanent peace must be conceived solely as an instrumentality of justice, unassociated with the passions of yesterday, and not so constituted as to attempt the dual functions of a political instrument of the conquerors and of an agency of peace. There can be no prosperity for the fundamental purposes sought to be achieved by any such association so long as it is an organ of any particular treaty, or committed to the attainment of the special aims of any nation or group of nations.

The American aspiration, indeed, the world aspiration, was an association of nations, based upon the application of justice and right, binding us in conference and cooperation for the prevention of war and pointing the way to a higher civilization and international fraternity in which all the world might share. In rejecting the league covenant and uttering that rejection to our own people, and to the world, we make no surrender of our hope and aim for an association to promote peace in which we would most heartily join. We wish it to be conceived in peace and dedicated to peace, and will relinquish no effort to bring the nations of the world into such fellowship, not in the surrender of national sovereignty but rejoicing in a nobler exercise of it in the advancement of human activities, amid the compensations of peaceful achievement.

In the national referendum to which I have adverted we pledged our efforts toward such association, and the pledge will be faithfully kept. In the plight of policy and performance, we told the American people we meant to seek an early establishment of peace. The United States alone among the allied and associated powers continues in a technical state of war against the Central Powers of Europe. This anomalous condition ought not to be permitted to continue. To establish the state of technical peace without further delay, I should approve a declaratory resolution by Congress to that effect, with the qualifications essential to protect all our rights. Such action would be the simplest keeping of faith with ourselves, and could in no sense be construed as a desertion of those with whom we shared our sacrifices in war, for these powers are already at peace.

Such a resolution should undertake to do no more than thus to declare the state of peace, which all America craves. It must add no difficulty in effecting, with just reparations, the restoration for which all Europe yearns, and upon which the world's recovery must be founded. Neither former enemy nor ally can mistake America's position, because our attitude as to responsibility for the war and the necessity for just reparations already has had formal and very earnest expression.

It would be unwise to undertake to make a statement of future policy with respect to European affairs in such a declaration of a state of peace. In correcting the failure of the Executive, in negotiating the most important treaty in the history of the Nation, to recognize the constitutional powers of the Senate we would go to the other extreme, equally objectionable, if Congress or the Senate should assume the function of the Executive. Our highest duty is the preservation of the constituted powers of each, and the promotion of the spirit of cooperation so essential to our common welfare.

It would be idle to declare for separate treaties of peace with the Central Powers on the assumption that these alone would be adequate, because the situation is so involved that our peace engagements cannot ignore the Old World relationship and the settlements already effected, nor is it desirable to do so in preserving our own rights and contracting our future relationships.

The wiser course would seem to be the acceptance of the confirmation of our rights and interests as already provided and to engage under the existing treaty, assuming, of course, that this can be satisfactorily accomplished by such explicit reservations and modifications as will secure our absolute freedom from inadvisable commitments and safeguard all our essential interests.

Neither Congress nor the people needs my assurance that a request to negotiate needed treaties of peace would be as superfluous and unnecessary as it is technically ineffective, and I know in my own heart there is none who would wish to embarrass the Executive in the performance of his duty when we are all so eager to turn disappointment and delay into gratifying accomplishment.

Problems relating to our foreign relations bear upon the present and the future and are of such a nature that the all-important future must be deliberately considered with greater concern than mere immediate relief from unhappy conditions. We have witnessed, yea, we have participated in the supremely tragic episode of war, but our deeper concern is in the continuing life of nations and the development of civilization.

We must not allow our vision to be impaired by the conflict among ourselves. The weariness at home and the disappointment to the world have been compensated in the proof that this Republic will surrender none of the heritage of nationality, but our rights in international relationship have to be asserted; they require establishment in compacts of amity; our part in readjustment and restoration cannot be ignored, and must be defined.

With the supergoverning league definitely rejected and with the world so informed, and with the status of peace proclaimed at home, we may proceed to negotiate the covenanted relationships so essential to the recognition of all the rights everywhere of our own Nation and play our full part in joining the peoples of the world in the pursuits of peace once more. Our obligations in effecting European tranquility, because of war's involvements, are not less impelling than our part in the war itself. This restoration must be wrought before the human procession can go onward again. We can be helpful because we are moved by no hatreds and harbor no fears. Helpfulness does not mean entanglement, and participation in economic adjustments does not mean sponsorship for treaty commitments which do not concern us, and in which we will have no part.

In an all-impelling wish to do the most and best for our own Republic and maintain its high place among nations and at the same time make the fullest offering of justice to them, I shall invite in the most practical way the advice of the Senate, after acquainting it with all the conditions to be met and obligations to be discharged, along with our own rights to be safeguarded. Prudence in making the program and confident cooperation in making it effective cannot lead us far astray. We can render no effective service to humanity until we prove anew our own capacity for cooperation in the coordination of powers contemplated in the Constitution, and no covenants which ignore our associations in the war can be made for the future. More, no helpful society of nations can be founded on justice and committed to peace until the covenants reestablishing peace are sealed by the nations which were at war. To such accomplishment—to the complete reestablishment of peace and its contracted relationships, to the realization of our aspirations for nations associated for world helpfulness without world government, for world stability on which humanity's hopes are founded—we shall address ourselves, fully mindful of the high privilege and the paramount duty of the United States in this critical period of the world.

IMMIGRATION LIMITATION ACT
May 19, 1921

By this act, quotas were placed for the first time upon the numbers of immigrants who might enter the United States.

Be it enacted by the Senate and House of Representatives of the United States of America in Congress assembled, That as used, in this Act—

The term "United States" means the United States, and any waters, territory, or other place subject to the jurisdiction thereof except the Canal Zone and the Philippine Islands; but if any alien leaves the Canal Zone or any insular possession of the United States and attempts to enter any other place under the jurisdiction of the United States nothing contained in this Act shall be construed as permitting him to enter under any other conditions than those applicable to all aliens.

The word "alien" includes any person not a native-born or naturalized citizen of the United States, but this definition shall not be held to include Indians of the United States not taxed nor citizens of the islands under the jurisdiction of the United States.

The term "Immigration Act" means the Act of February 5, 1917, entitled "An Act to regulate the immigration of aliens to, and the residence of aliens in, the United States"; and the term "immigration laws" includes such Act and all laws, conventions, and treaties of the United States relating to the immigration, exclusion, or expulsion of aliens.

Sec. 2. (a) That the number of aliens of any nationality who may be admitted under the immigration laws to the United States in any fiscal year shall be limited to 3 per centum of the number of foreign-born persons of such nationality resident in the United States as determined by the United States census of 1910. This provision shall not apply to the following, and they shall not be counted in reckoning any of the percentage limits provided in this Act: (1) Government officials, their families, attendants, servants, and employees; (2) aliens in continuous transit through the United States; (3) aliens lawfully admitted to the United States who later go in transit from one part of the United States to another through foreign contiguous territory; (4) aliens visiting the United States as tourists or temporarily for business or pleasure; (5) aliens from countries immigration from which is regulated in accordance with treaties or agreements relating solely to immigration; (6) aliens from the so-called Asiatic barred zone, as described in section 3 of the Immigration Act; (7) aliens who have resided continuously for at least one year immediately preceding the time of their admission to the United States in the Dominion of Canada, Newfoundland, the Republic of Cuba, the Republic of Mexico, countries of Central or South America, or adjacent islands; or (8) aliens under the age of eighteen who are children of citizens of the United States.

(b) For the purposes of this Act nationality shall be determined by country of birth, treating as separate countries the colonies or dependencies for which enumeration was made in the United States census of 1910.

(c) The Secretary of State, the Secretary of Commerce, and the Secretary of Labor, jointly, shall, as soon as feasible after the enactment of this Act, prepare a statement showing the number of persons of the various nationalities resident in the United States as determined by the United States census of 1910, which statement shall be the population basis for the purposes of this Act. In case of changes in political boundaries in foreign countries occurring subsequent to 1910 and resulting (1) in the creation of new countries, the Governments of which are recognized by the United States, or (2) in the transfer of territory from one country to another, such transfer being recognized by the United States, such officials, jointly, shall estimate the number of persons resident in the United States in 1910 who were born within the area included in such new countries or in such territory so transferred, and revise the population basis as to each country involved in such change of political boundary. For the purpose of such revision and for the purposes of this Act generally aliens born in the area included in any such new country shall be considered as having been born in such country, and aliens born in any territory so transferred shall be considered as having been born in the country to which such territory was transferred.

(d) When the maximum number of aliens of any nationality who may be admitted in any fiscal year under this Act shall have been admitted all other aliens of such nationality, except as otherwise provided in this Act, who may apply for admission during the same fiscal year shall be excluded: *Provided*, That the number of aliens of any nationality who may be admitted in any month shall not exceed 20 per centum of the total number of aliens of such nationality who are admissible in that fiscal year: *Provided further*, That aliens returning from a temporary visit abroad, aliens who are professional actors, artists, lecturers, singers, nurses, ministers of any religious denomination, professors for colleges or seminaries, aliens belonging to any recognized learned profession, or aliens employed as domestic servants, may, if otherwise admissible, be admitted notwithstanding the maximum number of aliens of the same nationality admissible in the same month or fiscal year, as the case may be, shall have entered the United States; but aliens of the classes included in this proviso who enter the United States before such maximum number shall have entered shall (unless excluded by subdivision (a) from being counted) be counted in reckoning the percentage limits provided in this Act: *Provided further*, That in the enforcement of this Act preference shall be given so far as possible to the wives, parents, brothers, sisters, children under eighteen years of age, and fiancees, (1) of citizens of the

United States, (2) of aliens now in the United States who have applied for citizenship in the manner provided by law, or (3) of persons eligible to United States citizenship who served in the military or naval forces of the United States at any time between April 6, 1917, and November 11, 1918, both dates inclusive, and have been separated from such forces under honorable conditions. . . .

Sec. 5. That this Act shall take effect and be enforced 15 days after its enactment (except sections 1 and 3 and subdivisions (b) and (c) of section 2, which shall take effect immediately upon the enactment of this Act), and shall continue in force until June 30, 1922, and the number of aliens of any nationality who may be admitted during the remaining period of the current fiscal year, from the date when this Act becomes effective to June 30, shall be limited in proportion to the number admissible during the fiscal year 1922.

Approved, May 19, 1921.

BUDGET AND ACCOUNTING ACT
June 10, 1921

In his message to Congress at the opening of the session, Harding had called for early enactment of legislation establishing a national budget system.

TITLE I.—DEFINITIONS.

Section 1. This Act may be cited as the "Budget and Accounting Act, 1921"....

TITLE II.—THE BUDGET.

Sec. 201. The President shall transmit to Congress on the first day of each regular session, the Budget, which shall set forth in summary and in detail:

(a) Estimates of the expenditures and appropriations necessary in his judgment for the support of the Government for the ensuing fiscal year; except that the estimates for such year for the Legislative Branch of the Government and the Supreme Court of the United States shall be transmitted to the President on or before October 15th of each year, and shall be included by him in the Budget without revision;

(b) His estimates of the receipts of the Government during the ensuing fiscal year, under (1) laws existing at the time the Budget is transmitted and also (2) under the revenue proposals, if any, contained in the Budget;

(c) The expenditures and receipts of the Government during the last completed fiscal year;

(d) Estimates of the expenditures and receipts of the Government during the fiscal year in progress....

Sec. 207. There is hereby created in the Treasury Department a Bureau to be known as the Bureau of the Budget. There shall be in the Bureau a Director and an Assistant Director, who shall be appointed by the President and receive salaries of $10,000 and $7,500 a year, respectively. The Assistant Director shall perform such duties as the Director may designate, and during the absence or incapacity of the Director or during a vacancy in the office of Director he shall act as Director. The Bureau, under such rules and regulations as the President may prescribe, shall prepare for him the Budget, the alternative Budget, and any supplemental or deficiency estimates, and to this end shall have authority to assemble, correlate, revise, reduce, or increase the estimates of the several departments or establishments.

Sec. 208. (a) The Director, under such rules and regulations as the President may prescribe, shall appoint and fix the compensation of attorneys and other employees and make expenditures for rent in the District of Columbia, printing, binding, telegrams, telephone service, law books, books of reference, periodicals, stationery, furniture, office equipment, other supplies, and necessary expenses of the office, within the appropriations made therefor. . . .

Sec. 209. The Bureau, when directed by the President, shall make a detailed study of the departments and establishments for the purpose of enabling the President to determine what changes (with a view of securing greater economy and efficiency in the conduct of the public service) should be made in (1) the existing organization, activities, and methods of business of such departments or establishments, (2) the appropriations therefor, (3) the assignment of particular activities to particular services, or (4) the regrouping of services. The results of such study shall be embodied in a report or reports to the President, who may transmit to Congress such report or reports or any part thereof with his recommendations on the matters covered thereby.

Sec. 210. The Bureau shall prepare for the President a codification of all laws or parts of laws relating to the preparation and transmission to Congress of statements of receipts and expenditures of the Government and of estimates of appropriations. The President shall transmit the same to Congress on or before the first Monday in December, 1921, with a recommendation as to the changes which, in his opinion, should be made in such laws or parts of laws. . . .

Sec. 212. The Bureau shall, at the request of any committee of either House of Congress having jurisdiction over revenue or appropriations, furnish the committee such aid and information as it may request.

Sec. 213. Under such regulations as the President may prescribe, (1) every department and establishment shall furnish to the Bureau such information as the Bureau may from time to time require, and (2) the Director and the Assistant Director, or any employee of the Bureau when duly authorized, shall, for the purpose of securing such information, have access to, and the right to examine, any books, documents, papers, or records of any such department or establishment.

Sec. 214. (a) The head of each department and establishment shall designate an official thereof as budget officer therefor, who, in each year under his direction and on or before a date fixed by him, shall prepare the departmental estimates. . . .

Sec. 215. The head of each department and establishment shall revise the departmental estimates and submit them to the Bureau on or before September 15 of each year. In case of his failure so to do, the President shall cause to be prepared such estimates and data as are necessary to enable him to include in the Budget estimates and statements in respect to the work of such department or establishment. . . .

TITLE III.—GENERAL ACCOUNTING OFFICE.

Sec. 301. There is created an establishment of the Government to be known as the General Accounting Office, which shall be independent of the executive departments and under the control and direction of the Comptroller General of the United States. The offices of Comptroller of the Treasury and Assistant Comptroller of the Treasury are abolished, to take effect July 1, 1921. All other officers and employees of the office of the Comptroller of the Treasury shall become officers and employees in the General Accounting Office at their grades and salaries on July 1, 1921, and all books, records, documents, papers, furniture, office equipment and other property of the office of the Comptroller of the Treasury shall become the property of the General Accounting Office. The Comptroller General is authorized to adopt a seal for the General Accounting Office.

Sec. 302. There shall be in the General Accounting Office a Comptroller General of the United States and an Assistant Comptroller General of the United States, who shall be appointed by the President with the advice and consent of the Senate, and shall receive salaries of $10,000 and $7,500 a year, respectively. The Assistant Comptroller General shall perform such duties as may be assigned to him by the Comptroller General, and during the absence or incapacity of the Comptroller General, or during a vacancy in that office, shall act as Comptroller General.

Sec. 303. Except as hereinafter provided in this section, the Comptroller General and the Assistant Comptroller General shall hold office for fifteen years. The Comptroller General shall not be eligible for reappointment. The Comptroller General or the Assistant Comptroller General may be removed at any time by joint resolution of Congress after notice and hearing, when, in the judgment of Congress, the Comptroller General or Assistant Comptroller General has become permanently incapacitated or has been inefficient, or guilty of neglect of duty, or of malfeasance in office, or of any felony or conduct involving moral turpitude, and for no other cause and in no other manner except by impeachment. Any Comptroller General or Assistant Comptroller General removed in the manner herein provided shall be ineligible for reappointment to that office. When a Comptroller General or Assistant Comptroller General attains the age of seventy years, he shall be retired from his office.

Sec. 304. All powers and duties now conferred or imposed by law upon the Comptroller of the Treasury or the six auditors of the Treasury Department, and the duties of the Division of Bookkeeping and Warrants of the Office of the Secretary of the Treasury relating to keeping the personal ledger accounts of disbursing and collecting officers, shall, so far as not inconsistent with this Act, be vested in and imposed upon the General Accounting Office and be exercised without direction from any other officer. . . .

The administrative examination of the accounts and vouchers of the Postal Service now imposed by law upon the Auditor for the Post Office Department shall be performed on and after July 1, 1921, by a bureau in the Post Office Department to be known as the Bureau of Accounts, which is hereby established for that purpose. The Bureau of Accounts shall be under the direction of a Comptroller, who shall be appointed by the President with the advice and consent of the Senate, and shall receive a salary of $5,000 a year....

Sec. 305. Section 236 of the Revised Statutes is amended to read as follows: "Sec. 236. All claims and demands whatever by the Government of the United States or against it, and all accounts whatever in which the Government of the United States is concerned, either as debtor or creditor, shall be settled and adjusted in the General Accounting Office." . . .

Sec. 309. The Comptroller General shall prescribe the forms, systems, and procedure for administrative appropriation and fund accounting in the several departments and establishments, and for the administrative examination of fiscal officers' accounts and claims against the United States.

Sec. 310. The offices of the six auditors shall be abolished, to take effect July 1, 1921. All other officers and employees of these offices except as otherwise provided herein shall become officers and employees of the General Accounting Office at their grades and salaries on July 1, 1921. . . .

Sec. 312.(a) The Comptroller General shall investigate, at the seat of government or elsewhere, all matters relating to the receipt, disbursement, and application of public funds, and shall make to the President when requested by him, and to Congress at the beginning of each regular session, a report in writing of the work of the General Accounting Office, containing recommendations concerning the legislation he may deem necessary to facilitate the prompt and accurate rendition and settlement of accounts and concerning such other matters relating to the receipt, disbursement, and application of public funds as he may think advisable. In such regular report, or in special reports at any time when Congress is in session, he shall make recommendations looking to greater economy or efficiency in public expenditures.

(b) He shall make such investigations and reports as shall be ordered by either House of Congress or by any committee of either House having jurisdiction over revenue, appropriations, or expenditures. The Comptroller General shall also, at the request of any such committee, direct assistants from his office to furnish the committee such aid and information as it may request.

(c) The Comptroller General shall specially report to Congress every expenditure or contract made by any department or establishment in any year in violation of law.

(d) He shall submit to Congress reports upon the adequacy and effectiveness of the administrative examination of accounts and claims in the respective departments and establishments and upon the adequacy and effectiveness of departmental inspection of the offices and accounts of fiscal officers.

(e) He shall furnish such information relating to expenditures and accounting to the Bureau of the Budget as it may request from time to time.

Sec. 313. All departments and establishments shall furnish to the Comptroller General such information regarding the powers, duties, activities, organization, financial transactions, and methods of business of their respective offices as he may from time to time require of them; and the Comptroller General, or any of his assistants or employees, when duly authorized by him, shall, for the purpose of securing such information, have access to and the right to examine any books, documents, papers, or records of any such department or establishment. The authority contained in this section shall not be applicable to expenditures made under the provisions of section 291 of the Revised Statutes.

Sec. 314. The Civil Service Commission shall establish an eligible register for accountants for the General Accounting Office, and the examinations of applicants for entrance upon such register shall be based upon questions approved by the Comptroller General. . . .

Approved, June 10, 1921.

END OF WAR DECLARED
July 2, 1921

The United States was the only Allied power still technically at war with the former Central Powers. Treaties with Germany and Austria were ratified in November.

Resolved by the Senate and House of Representatives of the United States of America in Congress assembled, That the state of war declared to exist between the Imperial German Government and the United States of America by the joint resolution of Congress approved April 6, 1917, is hereby declared at an end.

Sec. 2. That in making this declaration, and as a part of it, there are expressly reserved to the United States of America and its nationals any and all rights, privileges, indemnities, reparations, or advantages, together with the right to enforce the same, to which it or they have become entitled under the terms of the armistice signed November 11, 1918, or any extensions or modifications thereof; or which were acquired by or are in the possession of the United States of America by reason of its participation in the war or to which its nationals have thereby become rightfully entitled; or which, under the treaty of Versailles, have been stipulated for its or their benefit; or to which it is entitled as one of the principal allied and associated powers; or to which it is entitled by virtue of any Act or Acts of Congress; or otherwise.

Sec. 3. That the state of war declared to exist between the Imperial and Royal Austro-Hungarian Government and the United States of America by the joint resolution of Congress approved December 7, 1917, is hereby declared at an end.

Sec. 4. That in making this declaration, and as a part of it, there are expressly reserved to the United States of America and its nationals any and all rights, privileges, indemnities, reparations, or advantages, together with the right to enforce the same, to which it or they have become entitled under the terms of the armistice signed November 3, 1918, or any extensions or modifications thereof; or which were acquired by or are in the possession of the United States of America by reason of its participation in the war or to which its nationals have thereby become rightfully entitled; or which, under the treaty of Saint Germain-en-Laye or the treaty of Trianon, have been stipulated for its or their benefit; or to which it is entitled as one of the principal allied and associated powers; or to which it is entitled by virtue of any Act or Acts of Congress; or otherwise.

Sec. 5. All property of the Imperial German Government, or its successor or successors, and of all German nationals which was, on April 6, 1917, in or has since that date come into the possession or under control of, or has been the subject of a demand by the United States of America or of any of its officers, agents, or employees, from any source or by any agency whatsoever, and all property of the Imperial and Royal Austro-Hungarian Government, or its successor or successors, and of all Austro-Hungarian nationals which was on December 7, 1917, in or has since that date come into the possession or under control of, or has been the subject of a demand by the United States of America and no disposition thereof made, except as shall have been heretofore or specifically hereafter shall be provided by law until such time as the Imperial German Government and the Imperial and Royal Austro-Hungarian Government, or their successor or successors, shall have respectively made suitable provision for the satisfaction of all claims against said Governments respectively, of all persons, wheresoever domiciled, who owe permanent allegiance to the United States of America and who have suffered, through the acts of the Imperial German Government, or its agents, or the Imperial and Royal Austro-Hungarian Government, or its agents, since July 31, 1914, loss, damage, or injury to their persons or property, directly or indirectly, whether through the ownership of shares of stock in German, Austro-Hungarian, American, or other corporations, or in consequence of hostilities or of any operations of war, or otherwise, and also shall have granted to persons owing permanent allegiance to the United States of America most-favored-nation treatment, whether the same be national or otherwise, in all matters affecting residence, business, profession, trade, navigation, commerce and industrial property rights, and until the Imperial German Government and the Imperial and Royal Austro-Hungarian Government, or their successor or successors, shall have respectively confirmed to the United States of America all fines, forfeitures, penalties, and seizures imposed or made by the United States of America during the war, whether in respect to the property of the Imperial German Government or German nationals or the Imperial and Royal Austro-Hungarian Government or Austro-Hungarian nationals, and shall have waived any and all pecuniary claims against the United States of America.

Sec. 6. Nothing herein contained shall be construed to repeal, modify or amend the provisions of the joint resolution "declaring that certain Acts of Congress, joint resolutions and proclamations shall be construed as if the war had ended and the present or existing emergency expired," approved March 3, 1921, or the passport control provisions of an Act entitled "An act making appropriations for the diplomatic and consular service for the fiscal year ending June 30, 1922," approved March 2, 1921; nor to be effective to terminate the military status of any person now in desertion from the military or naval service of the United States, nor to terminate the liability to prosecution and punishment under the Selective Service law, approved May 18, 1917, of any person who failed to comply with the provisions of said Act, or of Acts amendatory thereof.

Approved, July 2, 1921.

NAVAL APPROPRIATION ACT
July 12, 1921

*Attached to the annual appropriation bill was authorization to
invite foreign governments to a disarmament conference.*

. . .Sec. 9. That the President is authorized and requested to invite the
Governments of Great Britain and Japan to send representatives to a
conference, which shall be charged with the duty of promptly entering into an
understanding or agreement by which the naval expenditures and building
programs of each of said Governments, to wit, the United States, Great
Britain, and Japan, shall be substantially reduced annually during the next
five years to such an extent and upon such terms as may be agreed
upon, which understanding or agreement is to be reported to the respective
Governments for approval.

Approved, July 12, 1921.

VETERANS BUREAU ESTABLISHED
August 9, 1921

*Consolidation of all veteran affairs under one bureau was designed
as a step in efficiency. At the end of 1922, evidence of graft and
mismanagement in the new bureau began to surface.*

TITLE I.—VETERANS' BUREAU.

Section 1. There is hereby established an independent bureau under the
President to be known as the Veterans' Bureau, the director of which shall be
appointed by the President, by and with the advice and consent of the
Senate. The director of the Veterans' Bureau shall receive a salary of
$10,000 per annum, payable monthly.

The word "director," as hereinafter used in this Act, shall mean the
Director of the Veterans' Bureau.

The powers and duties pertaining to the office of the Director of the
Bureau of War Risk Insurance now in the Treasury Department are hereby
transferred to the director, subject to the general direction of the
President, and the said office of the Director of the Bureau of War Risk
Insurance is hereby abolished.

There shall be included on the technical and administrative staff of the
director such staff officers, experts, and assistants as the director shall
prescribe; and there shall be in the Veterans' Bureau such sections and
subdivisions thereof as the director shall prescribe.

Sec. 2. The director, subject to the general direction of the President, shall
administer, execute, and enforce the provisions of this Act, and for that
purpose shall have full power and authority to make rules and regulations not
inconsistent with the provisions of this Act, which are necessary or
appropriate to carry out its purposes and shall decide all questions arising
under this Act except as otherwise provided herein.

Sec. 3. The functions, powers, and duties conferred by existing law upon
the Bureau of War Risk Insurance are hereby transferred to and made a part
of the Veterans' Bureau.

Sec. 4. All personnel, facilities, property, and equipment, including
leases, contracts, and other obligations and instrumentalities in the District of
Columbia and elsewhere of the Bureau of War Risk Insurance, of the United
States Public Health Service, as described and provided in a written order of
the Treasury Department issued and signed by the Secretary of the Treasury
on April 19, 1921, and designated "Order relative to the transfer of certain
activities of the United States Public Health Service, relating to the Bureau of
War Risk Insurance, including the trainees of the Rehabilitation Division of

the Federal Board for Vocational Education," and of the Rehabilitation Division of the Federal Board for Vocational Education, as a result of the administration of the Act approved June 27, 1918, and amendments thereto, are hereby transferred to and made a part of the Veterans' Bureau under the control, management, operation, and supervision of the director, and subject to such change in designation and organization as he may deem necessary in carrying out the provisions of this Act: *Provided*, That all commissioned personnel detailed or hereafter detailed from the United States Public Health Service to the Veterans' Bureau, shall hold the same rank and grade, shall receive the same pay and allowances, and shall be subject to the same rules for relative rank and promotion as now or hereafter may be provided by law for commissioned personnel of the same rank or grade or performing the same or similar duties in the United States Public Health Service. . . .

Sec. 6. The director shall establish a central office in the District of Columbia, and not more than fourteen regional offices and such suboffices, not exceeding one hundred and forty in number, within the territory of the United States and its outlying possessions as may be deemed necessary by him and in the best interests of the work committed to the Veterans' Bureau and to carry out the purposes of this Act. Such regional offices may, pending final action by the director in case of an appeal, under such rules and regulations as may be prescribed by the director, exercise such powers for hearing complaints and for examining, rating, and awarding compensation claims, granting medical, surgical, dental, and hospital care, convalescent care, and necessary and reasonable after care, making insurance awards, granting vocational training, and all other matters delegated to them by the director as could be performed lawfully under this Act by the central office. The suboffices shall have such powers as may be delegated to them by the director, except to make compensation and insurance awards and to grant vocational training. . . .

Sec. 7. The beneficiaries of the Bureau of War Risk Insurance and the Rehabilitation Division of the Federal Board for Vocational Education shall hereafter be the beneficiaries of the Veterans' Bureau, and complete individual record of each beneficiary shall be kept by the Veterans' Bureau. . . .

ApprovedAugust 9, 1921.

OPENING OF ARMS CONFERENCE
November 12, 1921

Harding, in this opening address at the Washington Disarmament Conference, was speaking to top representatives of nine powers: The United States, Great Britain, Japan, Italy, France, China, the Netherlands, Portugal and Belgium. The latter four countries had been invited because of national interests in Asian affairs.

Mr. Secretary and members of the conference, ladies, and gentlemen, it is a great and happy privilege to bid the delegates to this conference a cordial welcome to the Capital of the United States of America. It is not only a satisfaction to greet you because we were lately participants in a common cause, in which shared sacrifices and sorrows and triumphs brought our nations more closely together, but it is gratifying to address you as the spokesmen for nations whose convictions and attending actions have so much to do with the weal or woe of all mankind.

It is not possible to overappraise the importance of such a conference. It is no unseemly boast, no disparagement of other nations which, though not represented, are held in highest respect, to declare that the conclusions of this body will have a signal influence on all human progress—on the fortunes of the world.

Here is a meeting, I can well believe, which is an earnest of the awakened conscience of twentieth century civilization. It is not a convention of remorse nor a session of sorrow. It is not the conference of victors to define terms of settlement. Nor is it a council of nations seeking to remake humankind. It is rather a coming together, from all parts of the earth, to apply the better attributes of mankind to minimize the faults in our international relationships.

Speaking as official sponsor for the invitation, I think I may say the call is not of the United States of America alone; it is rather the spoken word of a war-wearied world, struggling for restoration, hungering and thirsting for better relationship; of humanity crying for relief and craving assurances of lasting peace.

It is easy to understand this world-wide aspiration. The glory of triumph, the rejoicing in achievement, the love of liberty, the devotion to country, the pangs of sorrow, the burdens of debt, the desolation of ruin—all these are appraised alike in all lands. Here in the United States we are but freshly turned from the burial of an unknown American soldier, when a Nation sorrowed while paying him tribute. Whether it was spoken or not, a hundred millions of our people were summarizing the inexcusable causes, the incalculable cost, the unspeakable sacrifices, and the unutterable sorrows, and there was the ever-impelling question: How can humanity justify or God forgive? Human hate demands no such toll; ambition and greed must be denied it. If misunderstanding must take the blame, then let us banish it, and let understanding rule and make good will regnant everywhere. All of us demand liberty and justice. There cannot be one without the other, and they must be held the unquestioned possession of all peoples. Inherent rights are of God, and the tragedies of the world originate in their attempted denial. The world today is infringing their enjoyment by arming to defend or deny, when simple sanity calls for their recognition through common understanding.

Out of the cataclysm of the World War came new fellowships, new convictions, new aspirations. It is ours to make the most of them. A world staggering with debt needs its burden lifted. Humanity which has been shocked by wanton destruction would minimize the agencies of that destruction. Contemplating the measureless cost of war and the continuing burden of armament, all thoughtful peoples wish for real limitation of armament and would like war outlawed. In soberest reflection the world's hundreds of millions who pay in peace and die in war wish their statesmen to turn the expenditures for destruction into means of construction, aimed at a higher state for those who live and follow after.

It is not alone that the world cannot readjust itself and cast aside the excess burdens without relief from the leaders of men. War has grown progressively cruel and more destructive from the first recorded conflict to this pregnant day, and the reverse order would more become our boasted civilization.

Gentlemen of the conference, the United States welcomes you with unselfish hands. We harbor no fears; we have no sordid ends to serve; we suspect no enemy; we contemplate or apprehend no conquests. Content with what we have, we seek nothing which is another's. We only wish to do with you that finer, nobler thing which no nations can do alone.

We wish to sit with you at the table of international understanding and good will. In good conscience we are eager to meet you frankly, and invite and offer cooperation. The world demands a sober contemplation of the existing order and the realization that there can be no cure without sacrifice, not by one of us, but by all of us.

I do not mean surrendered rights, or narrowed freedom, or denied aspirations, or ignored national necessities. Our Republic would no more ask for these than it would give. No pride need be humbled, no nationality submerged, but I would have a mergence of minds committing all of us to less preparation for war and more enjoyment of fortunate peace.

The higher hopes come of the spirit of our coming together. It is but just to recognize varying needs and peculiar positions. Nothing can be accomplished in disregard of national apprehensions. Rather, we should act together to remove the causes of apprehensions. This is not to be done in intrigue. Greater assurance is found in the exchanges of simple honesty and directness, among men resolved to accomplish as becomes leaders among nations, when civilization itself has come to its crucial test.

It is not to be challenged that government fails when the excess of its cost robs the people of the way to happiness and the opportunity to achieve. If the finer sentiments were not urging, the cold, hard facts of excessive cost and the eloquence of economics would urge us to reduce our armaments. If the concept of a better order does not appeal, then let us ponder the burden and the blight of continued competition.

It is not to be denied that the world has swung along throughout the ages without heeding this call from the kindlier hearts of men. But the same world never before was so tragically brought to realization of the utter futility of passion's sway when reason and conscience and fellowship point a nobler way.

I can speak officially only for our United States. Our hundred millions frankly want less of armament and none of war. Wholly free from guile, sure in our own minds that we harbor no unworthy designs, we accredit the world with the same good intent. So I welcome you, not alone in good will and high purpose, but with high faith.

We are met for a service to mankind. In all simplicity, in all honesty and all honor, there may be written here the avowals of a world conscience refined by the consuming fires of war, and made more sensitive by the anxious aftermath. I hope for that understanding which will emphasize the guaranties of peace, and for commitments to less burdens and a better order which will tranquilize the world. In such an accomplishment there will be added glory to your flags and ours, and the rejoicing of mankind will make the transcending music of all succeeding time.

SECRETARY HUGHES CALLS FOR NAVAL DISARMAMENT
November 12, 1921

Charles E. Hughes, U.S. Secretary of State, was named presiding officer of the Washington Disarmament Conference. Hughes' detailed knowledge of naval armament and construction plans of the other countries amazed and dismayed their representatives. His dramatic call for naval disarmament startled the world.

Gentlemen, it is with a deep sense of privilege and responsibility that I accept the honor you have conferred.

Permit me to express the most cordial appreciation of the assurances of friendly cooperation which have been generously expressed by the representatives of all the invited Governments. The earnest desire and purpose, manifested in every step in the approach to this meeting, that we should meet the reasonable expectation of a watching world by effective action suited to the opportunity is the best augury for the success of the conference.

The President invited the Governments of the British Empire, France, Italy, and Japan to participate in a conference on the subject of limitation of armament, in connection with which Pacific and Far Eastern questions would also be discussed. It would have been most agreeable to the President to have invited all the powers to take part in this conference, but it was thought to be a time when other considerations should yield to the practical requirements of the existing exigency, and in this view the invitation was extended to the group known as the principal allied and associated powers, which, by reason of the conditions produced by the war, control in the main the armament of the world. The opportunity to limit armament lies within their grasp.

It was recognized, however, that the interest of other powers in the Far East made it appropriate that they should be invited to participate in the discussion of Pacific and Far Eastern problems, and, with the approval of the five powers, an invitation to take part in the discussion of those questions has been extended to Belgium, China, the Netherlands, and Portugal.

The inclusion of the proposal for the discussion of Pacific and Far Eastern questions was not for the purpose of embarrassing or delaying an agreement for limitation of armament, but rather to support that undertaking by availing ourselves of this meeting to endeavor to reach a common understanding as to the principles and policies to be followed in the Far East and thus greatly to diminish, and if possible wholly to remove, discernible sources of controversy. It is believed that by interchanges of views at this opportune time the Governments represented here may find a basis of accord and thus give expression to their desire to assure enduring friendship.

In the public discussions which have preceded the conference there have been apparently two competing views; one, that the consideration of armament should await the result of the discussion of Far Eastern questions, and another, that the latter discussion should be postponed until an agreement for limitation of armament has been reached. I am unable to find sufficient reason for adopting either of these extreme views. I think that it would be most unfortunate if we should disappoint the hopes which have attached to this meeting by a postponement of the consideration of the first subject. The world looks to this conference to relieve humanity of the crushing burden created by competition in armament, and it is the view of the American Government that we should meet that expectation without any unnecessary delay. It is therefore proposed that the conference should proceed at once to consider the question of the limitation of armament.

This, however, does not mean that we must postpone the examination of Far Eastern questions. These questions of vast importance press for solution. It is hoped that immediate provision may be made to deal with them adequately, and it is suggested that it may be found to be entirely practicable through the distribution of the work among designated committees to make progress to the ends sought to be achieved without either subject being treated as a hindrance to the proper consideration and disposition of the other.

The proposal to limit armament by an agreement of the powers is not a new one, and we are admonished by the futility of earlier efforts. It may be well to recall the noble aspirations which were voiced 23 years ago in the imperial rescript of His Majesty the Emperor of Russia. It was then pointed out with clarity and emphasis that "The intellectual and physical strength of the nations, labor, and capital are for the major part diverted from their natural application and unproductively consumed. Hundreds of millions are devoted to acquiring terrible engines of destruction, which, though today regarded as the last word of science, are destined tomorrow to lose all value in consequence of some fresh discovery in the same field. National culture, economic progress, and the production of wealth are either paralyzed or checked in their development. Moreover, in proportion as the armaments of each power increase, so do they less and less fulfill the object which the Governments have set before themselves. The economic crises, due in great part to the system of armaments a l'outrance and the continual danger which lies in this massing of war materials, are transforming the armed peace of our days into a crushing burden, which the peoples have more and more difficulty in bearing. It appears evident, then, that if this state of things were prolonged it would inevitably lead to the calamity which it is desired to avert, and the horrors of which make every thinking man shudder in advance. To put an end to these incessant armaments and to seek the means of warding off the calamities which are threatening the whole world—such is the supreme duty which is today imposed on all States."

It was with this sense of obligation that His Majesty the Emperor of Russia proposed the conference, which was "to occupy itself with this grave problem" and which met at The Hague in the year 1899. Important as were the deliberations and conclusions of that conference, especially with respect to the pacific settlement of international disputes, its result in the specific matter of limitation of armament went no further than the adoption of a final resolution setting forth the opinion "that the restriction of military charges, which are at present a heavy burden on the world, is extremely desirable for the increase of the material and moral welfare of mankind," and the utterance of the wish that the Governments "may examine the possibility of an agreement as to the limitation of armed forces by land and sea, and of war budgets."

It was seven years later that the Secretary of State of the United States, Mr. Elihu Root, in answering a note of the Russian ambassador suggesting in outline a program of the second peace conference, said: "The Government of the United States, therefore, feels it to be its duty to reserve for itself the liberty to propose to the second peace conference, as one of the subjects for consideration, the reduction or limitation of armaments, in the hope that, if nothing further can be accomplished, some slight advance may be made toward the realization of the lofty conception which actuated the Emperor of Russia in calling the first conference." It is significant that the Imperial German Government expressed itself as "absolutely opposed to the question of disarmament" and that the Emperor of Germany threatened to decline to send delegates if the subject of disarmament was to be discussed. In view, however, of the resolution which had been adopted at the first Hague conference the delegates of the United States were instructed that the subject of limitation of armament "should be regarded as unfinished business, and that the second conference should ascertain and give full consideration to the results of such examination as the Governments may have given to the possibility of an agreement pursuant to the wish expressed by the first conference." But by reason of the obstacles which the subject had encountered, the second peace conference at The Hague, although it made notable progress in provision for the peaceful settlement of controversies, was unable to deal with limitation of armament except by a resolution in the following general terms: "The conference confirms the resolution adopted by the conference of 1899 in regard to the limitation of military expenditure; and inasmuch as military expenditure has considerably increased in almost every country since that time, the conference declares that it is eminently desirable that the Governments should resume the serious examination of this question."

This was the fruition of the efforts of eight years. Although the effect was clearly perceived, the race in preparation of armament, wholly unaffected by these futile suggestions, went on until it fittingly culminated in the greatest war of history; and we are now suffering from the unparalleled loss of life, the destruction of hopes, the economic dislocations, and the widespread impoverishment which measure the cost of the victory over the brutal pretensions of military force.

But if we are warned by the inadequacy of earlier endeavors for limitation of armament, we cannot fail to recognize the extraordinary opportunity now presented. We not only have the lessons of the past to guide us, not only do we have the reaction from the disillusioning experiences of war, but we must meet the challenge of imperative economic demands. What was convenient or highly desirable before is now a matter of vital necessity. If there is to be economic rehabilitation, if the longings for reasonable progress are not to be denied, if we are to be spared the uprisings of peoples made desperate in the desire to shake off burdens no longer endurable, competition in armament must stop. The present opportunity not only derives its advantage from a general appreciation of this fact, but the power to deal with the exigency now rests with a small group of nations, represented here, who have every reason to desire peace and to promote amity. The astounding ambition which lay athwart the promise of the second Hague conference no longer menaces the world, and the great opportunity of liberty-loving and peace-preserving democracies has come. Is it not plain that the time has passed for mere resolutions that the responsible powers should examine the question of limitation of armament? We can no longer content ourselves with investigations, with statistics, with reports, with the circumlocution of inquiry. The essential facts are sufficiently known. The time has come, and this conference has been called, not for general resolutions or mutual advice, but for action. We meet with full understanding that the aspirations of mankind are not to be defeated either by plausible suggestions of postponement or by impracticable counsels of perfection. Power and responsibility are here, and the world awaits a practicable program which shall at once be put into execution.

I am confident that I shall have your approval in suggesting that in this matter, as well as in others before the conference, it is desirable to follow the course of procedure which has the best promise of achievement rather than one which would facilitate division; and thus, constantly aiming to agree so far as possible, we shall, with each point of agreement, make it easier to proceed to others.

The question, in relation to armament, which may be regarded as of primary importance at this time, and with which we can deal most promptly and effectively, is the limitation of naval armament. There are certain general considerations which may be deemed pertinent to this subject.

The first is that the core of the difficulty is to be found in the competition in naval programs, and that, in order appropriately to limit naval armament, competition in its production must be abandoned. Competition will not be remedied by resolves with respect to the method of its continuance. One program inevitably leads to another, and if competition continues its regulation is impracticable. There is only one adequate way out and that is to end it now.

It is apparent that this cannot be accomplished without serious sacrifices. Enormous sums have been expended upon ships under construction and building programs which are now under way cannot be given up without heavy loss. Yet if the present construction of capital ships goes forward other ships will inevitably be built to rival them and this will lead to still others. Thus the race will continue so long as ability to continue lasts. The effort to escape sacrifices is futile. We must face them or yield our purpose.

It is also clear that no one of the naval powers should be expected to make these sacrifices alone. The only hope of limitation of naval armament is by agreement among the nations concerned, and this agreement should be entirely fair and reasonable in the extent of the sacrifices required of each of the powers. In considering the basis of such an agreement, and the commensurate sacrifices to be required, it is necessary to have regard to the existing naval strength of the great naval powers, including the extent of construction already effected in the case of ships in process. This follows from the fact that one nation is as free to compete as another, and each may find grounds for its action. What one may do another may demand the opportunity to rival, and we remain in the thrall of competitive effort. I may add that the American delegates are advised by their naval experts that the tonnage of capital ships may fairly be taken to measure the relative strength of navies, as the provision for auxiliary combatant craft should sustain a reasonable relation to the capital ship tonnage allowed.

It would also seem to be a vital part of a plan for the limitation of naval armament that there should be a naval holiday. It is proposed that for a period of not less than 10 years there should be no further construction of capital ships.

I am happy to say that I am at liberty to go beyond these general propositions, and on behalf of the American delegation, acting under the instructions of the President of the United States, to submit to you a concrete proposition for an agreement for the limitation of naval armament.

It should be added that this proposal immediately concerns the British Empire, Japan, and the United States. In view of the extraordinary conditions due to the World War affecting the existing strength of the navies of France and Italy, it is not thought to be necessary to discuss at this stage of the proceedings the tonnage allowance of these nations, but the United States proposes that this matter be reserved for the later consideration of the conference.

In making the present proposal the United States is most solicitous to deal with the question upon an entirely reasonable and practicable basis, to the end that the just interests of all shall be adequately guarded and that national security and defense shall be maintained. Four general principles have been applied:

(1) That all capital ship-building programs, either actual or projected, should be abandoned;

(2) That further reduction should be made through the scrapping of certain of the older ships;

(3) That in general regard should be had to the existing naval strength of the powers concerned;

(4) That the capital ship tonnage should be used as the measurement of strength for navies and a proportionate allowance of auxiliary combatant craft prescribed.

The principal features of the proposed agreement are as follows:

CAPITAL SHIPS

United States

The United States is now completing its program of 1916 calling for 10 new battleships and 6 battle cruisers. One battleship has been completed. The others are in various stages of construction; in some cases from 60 to over 80 per cent of the construction has been done. On these 15 capital ships now being built over $330,000,000 have been spent. Still the United States is willing in the interest of an immediate limitation of naval armament to scrap all these ships.

The United States proposes, if this plan is accepted—

(1) To scrap all capital ships now under construction. This includes 6 battle cruisers and 7 battleships on the ways and in course of building, and 2 battleships launched.

The total number of new capital ships thus to be scrapped is 15. The total tonnage of the new capital ships when completed would be 618,000 tons.

(2) To scrap all of the older battleships up to, but not including, the *Delaware* and *North Dakota*. The number of these old battleships to be scrapped is 15. Their total tonnage is 227,740 tons.

Thus the number of capital ships to be scrapped by the United States, if this plan is accepted, is 30, with an aggregate tonnage (including that of ships in construction, if completed) of 845,740 tons.

Great Britain

The plan contemplates that Great Britain and Japan shall take action which is fairly commensurate with this action on the part of the United States.

It is proposed that Great Britain—

(1) Shall stop further construction on the four new Hoods, the new capital

ships not laid down but upon which money has been spent. These four ships, if completed, would have tonnage displacement of 172,000 tons.

(2) Shall, in addition, scrap her predreadnaughts, second-line battleships, and first-line battleships up to, but not including, the *King George V* class.

These, with certain predreadnaughts which it is understood have already been scrapped, would amount to 19 capital ships and a tonnage reduction of 411,375 tons.

The total tonnage of ships thus to be scrapped by Great Britain (including the tonnage of the four Hoods, if completed) would be 583,375 tons.

Japan

It is proposed that Japan—

(1) Shall abandon her program of ships not yet laid down, viz, the *Kii, Owari, No. 7* and *No. 8 battleships*, and *Nos. 5, 6, 7,* and *8* battle cruisers.

It should be observed that this does not involve the stopping of construction, as the construction of none of these ships has been begun.

(2) Shall scrap 3 capital ships (the *Matsu* launched, the *Tosa,* and *Kago* in course of building) and four battle cruisers (the *Amagi* and *Akagi* in course of building, and the *Atoga* and *Takao* not yet laid down, but for which certain material has been assembled).

The total number of new capital ships to be scrapped under this paragraph is seven. The total tonnage of these new capital ships when completed would be 289,100 tons.

(3) Shall scrap all predreadnaughts and battleships of the second line. This would include the scrapping of all ships up to, but not including, the *Settsu*; that is, the scrapping of 10 older ships, with a total tonnage of 159,828 tons.

The total reduction of tonnage on vessels existing, laid down, or for which material has been assembled (taking the tonnage of the new ships when completed) would be 448,928 tons.

Thus, under this plan there would be immediately destroyed, of the navies of the three powers, 66 capital fighting ships, built and building, with a total tonnage of 1,878,043.

It is proposed that it should be agreed by the United States, Great Britain, and Japan that their navies, with respect to capital ships, within three months after the making of the agreement shall consist of certain ships designated in the proposal and numbering for the United States 18, for Great Britain 22, for Japan 10.

The tonnage of these ships would be as follows: Of the United States, 500,650; of Great Britain, 604,450; of Japan, 299,700. In reaching this result, the age factor in the case of the respective navies has received appropriate consideration.

REPLACEMENT

With respect to replacement, the United States proposes:

(1) That it be agreed that the first replacement tonnage shall not be laid down until 10 years from the date of the agreement;

(2) That replacement be limited by an agreed maximum of capital ship tonnage as follows:

For the United States--500,000 tons
For Great Britain--500,000 tons
For Japan---300,000 tons

(3) That subject to the 10-year limitation above fixed and the maximum standard, capital ships may be replaced when they are 20 years old by new capital ship construction;

(4) That no capital ship shall be built in replacement with a tonnage displacement of more than 35,000 tons.

I have sketched the proposal only in outline, leaving the technical details to be supplied by the formal proposition which is ready for submission to the delegates.

The plan includes provision for the limitation of auxiliary combatant craft. This term embraces three classes; that is (1) auxiliary surface combatant craft, such as cruisers (exclusive of battle cruisers), flotilla leaders, destroyers, and various surface types; (2) submarines; and (3) airplane carriers.

I shall not attempt to review the proposals for these various classes, as they bear a definite relation to the provisions for capital fighting ships.

With the acceptance of this plan the burden of meeting the demands of competition in naval armament will be lifted. Enormous sums will be released to aid the progress of civilization. At the same time the proper demands of national defense will be adequately met and the nations will have ample opportunity during the naval holiday of 10 years to consider their future course. Preparation for offensive naval war will stop now.

I shall not attempt at this time to take up the other topics which have been listed upon the tentative agenda proposed in anticipation of the conference.

FIRST ANNUAL MESSAGE
December 6, 1921

In this message, Harding continued his theme of a "return to normalcy," reviewing legislation needed to accomplish that aim.

Mr. Speaker and Members of the Congress: It is a very gratifying privilege to come to the Congress with the Republic at peace with all the nations of the world. More, it is equally gratifying to report that our country is not only free from every impending menace of war, but there are growing assurances of the permanency of the peace which we so deeply cherish.

For approximately ten years we have dwelt amid menaces of war or as participants in war's actualities, and the inevitable aftermath, with its disordered conditions, has added to the difficulties of government which adequately cannot be appraised except by those who are in immediate contact and know the responsibilities. Our tasks would be less difficult if we had only ourselves to consider, but so much of the world was involved, the disordered conditions are so well-nigh universal, even among nations not engaged in actual warfare, that no permanent readjustments can be effected without consideration of our inescapable relationship to world affairs in finance and trade. Indeed, we should be unworthy of our best traditions if we were unmindful of social, moral, and political conditions which are not of direct concern to us, but which do appeal to the human sympathies and the very becoming interest of a people blest with our national good fortune.

It is not my purpose to bring to you a program of world restoration. In the main such a program must be worked out by the nations more directly concerned. They must themselves turn to the heroic remedies for the menacing conditions under which they are struggling, then we can help, and we mean to help. We shall do so unselfishly because there is compensation in the consciousness of assisting, selfishly because the commerce and international exchanges in trade, which marked our high tide of fortunate advancement, are possible only when the nations of all continents are restored to stable order and normal relationship.

In the main the contribution of this Republic to restored normalcy in the world must come through the initiative of the executive branch of the Government, but the best of intentions and most carefully considered purposes would fail utterly if the sanction and the cooperation of Congress were not cheerfully accorded.

I am very sure we shall have no conflict of opinion about constitutional duties or authority. During the anxieties of war, when necessity seemed compelling, there were excessive grants of authority and an extraordinary concentration of powers in the Chief Executive. The repeal of war-time legislation and the automatic expirations which attended the peace proclamations have put an end to these emergency excesses, but I have the wish to go further than that. I want to join you in restoring, in the most cordial way, the spirit of coordination and cooperation, and that mutuality of confidence and respect which is necessary in representative popular government.

Encroachment upon the functions of Congress or attempted dictation of its policy are not to be thought of, much less attempted, but there is an insistent call for harmony of purpose and concord of action to speed the solution of the difficult problems confronting both the legislative and executive branches of the Government.

It is worthwhile to make allusion here to the character of our Government, mindful as one must be that an address to you is no less a message to all our people, for whom you speak most intimately. Ours is a popular Government through political parties. We divide along political lines, and I would ever have it so. I do not mean that partisan preferences should hinder any public servant in the performance of a conscientious and patriotic official duty. We saw partisan lines utterly obliterated when war imperiled, and our faith in the Republic was riveted anew. We ought not to find these partisan lines obstructing the expeditious solution of the urgent problems of peace.

Granting that we are fundamentally a representative popular Government, with political parties the governing agencies, I believe the political party in power should assume responsibility, determine upon policies in the conference which supplements conventions and election campaigns, and then strive for achievement through adherence to the accepted policy.

There is vastly greater security, immensely more of the national viewpoint, much larger and prompter accomplishment where our divisions are along party lines, in the broader and loftier sense, than to divide geographically, or according to pursuits, or personal following. For a century and a third, parties have been charged with responsibility and held to strict accounting. When they fail, they are relieved of authority; and the system has brought us to a national eminence no less than a world example.

Necessarily legislation is a matter of compromise. The full ideal is seldom attained. In that meeting of minds necessary to insure results, there must and will be accommodations and compromises, but in the estimate of convictions and sincere purposes the supreme responsibility to national interest must not be ignored. The shield to the high-minded public servant who adheres to party policy is manifest, but the higher purpose is the good of the Republic as a whole.

It would be ungracious to withhold acknowledgment of the really large volume and excellent quality of work accomplished by the extraordinary session of Congress which so recently adjourned. I am not unmindful of the very difficult tasks with which you were called to deal, and no one can ignore the insistent conditions which, during recent years, have called for the continued and almost exclusive attention of your membership to public work. It would suggest insincerity if I expressed complete accord with every expression recorded in your roll calls, but we are all agreed about the difficulties and the inevitable divergence of opinion in seeking the reduction, amelioration and readjustment of the burdens of taxation. Later on, when other problems are solved, I shall make some recommendations about renewed consideration of our tax program, but for the immediate time before us we must be content with the billion dollar reduction in the tax draft upon the people, and diminished irritations, banished uncertainty and improved methods of collection. By your sustainment of the rigid economies already inaugurated, with hoped-for extension of these economies and added efficiencies in administration, I believe further reductions may be enacted and hindering burdens abolished.

In these urgent economies we shall be immensely assisted by the budget system for which you made provision in the extraordinary session. The first budget is before you. Its preparation is a signal achievement, and the perfection of the system, a thing impossible in the few months available for its initial trial, will mark its enactment as the beginning of the greatest reformation in governmental practices since the beginning of the Republic.

There is pending a grant of authority to the administrative branch of the Government for the funding and settlement of our vast foreign loans growing out of our grant of war credits. With the hands of the executive branch held impotent to deal with these debts we are hindering urgent readjustments among our debtors and accomplishing nothing for ourselves. I think it is fair for the Congress to assume that the executive branch of the Government would adopt no major policy in dealing with these matters which would conflict with the purpose of Congress in authorizing the loans, certainly not without asking congressional approval, but there are minor problems incident to prudent loan transactions and the safeguarding of our interests which cannot even be attempted without this authorization. It will be helpful to ourselves and it will improve conditions among our debtors if funding and the settlement of defaulted interest may be negotiated.

The previous Congress, deeply concerned in behalf of our merchant marine, in 1920 enacted the existing shipping law, designed for the upbuilding of the American merchant marine. Among other things provided to encourage our shipping on the world's seas, the Executive was directed to give notice of the termination of all existing commercial treaties in order to admit of reduced duties on imports carried in American bottoms. During the life of the act no Executive has complied with this order of the Congress. When the present administration came into responsibility it began an early inquiry into the failure to execute the expressed purpose of the Jones Act. Only one conclusion has been possible. Frankly, Members of House and Senate, eager as I am to join you in the making of an American merchant marine commensurate with our commerce, the denouncement of our commercial treaties would involve us in a chaos of trade relationships and add indescribably to the confusion of the already disordered commercial world. Our power to do so is not disputed, but power and ships, without comity of relationship, will not give us the expanded trade which is inseparably linked with a great merchant marine. Moreover, the applied reduction of duty, for which the treaty denouncements were necessary, encouraged only the carrying of dutiable imports to our shores, while the tonnage which unfurls the flag on the seas is both free and dutiable, and the cargoes which make a nation eminent in trade are outgoing, rather than incoming.

It is not my thought to lay the problem before you in detail today. It is desired only to say to you that the executive branch of the Government, uninfluenced by the protest of any nation, for none has been made, is well convinced that your proposal, highly intended and heartily supported here, is so fraught with difficulties and so marked by tendencies to discourage trade expansion, that I invite your tolerance of noncompliance for only a few weeks until a plan may be presented which contemplates no greater draft upon the Public Treasury, and which, though yet too crude to offer it today, gives such promise of expanding our merchant marine, that it will argue its own approval. It is enough to say today that we are so possessed of ships, and the American intention to establish a merchant marine is so unalterable, that a plan of reimbursement, at no other cost than is contemplated in the existing act, will appeal to the pride and encourage the hope of all the American people.

There is before you the completion of the enactment of what has been termed a "permanent" tariff law, the word "permanent" being used to distinguish it from the emergency act which the Congress expedited early in the extraordinary session, and which is the law today. I cannot too strongly urge an early completion of this necessary legislation. It is needed to stabilize our industry at home; it is essential to make more definite our trade relations abroad. More, it is vital to the preservation of many of our own industries which contribute so notably to the very lifeblood of our Nation.

There is now, and there always will be, a storm of conflicting opinion about any tariff revision. We cannot go far wrong when we base our tariffs on the policy of preserving the productive activities which enhance employment and add to our national prosperity.

Again comes the reminder that we must not be unmindful of world conditions, that peoples are struggling for industrial rehabilitation and that we cannot dwell in industrial and commercial exclusion and at the same time do the just thing in aiding world reconstruction and readjustment. We do not seek a selfish aloofness, and we could not profit by it, were it possible. We recognize the necessity of buying wherever we sell, and the permanency of trade lies in its acceptable exchanges. In our pursuit of markets we must give as well as receive. We cannot sell to others who do not produce, nor can we buy unless we produce at home. Sensible of every obligation of humanity, commerce and finance, linked as they are in the present world condition, it is not to be argued that we need destroy ourselves to be helpful to others. With all my heart I wish restoration to the peoples blighted by the awful World War, but the process of restoration does not lie in our acceptance of like conditions. It were better to remain on firm ground, strive for ample employment and high standards of wage at home, and point the way to balanced budgets, rigid economies, and resolute, efficient work as the necessary remedies to cure disaster.

Everything relating to trade, among ourselves and among nations, has been expanded, excessive, inflated, abnormal, and there is a madness in finance which no American policy alone will cure. We are a creditor Nation, not by normal processes, but made so by war. It is not an unworthy selfishness to seek to save ourselves, when the processes of that salvation are not only not denied to others, but commended to them. We seek to undermine for others no industry by which they subsist; we are obligated to permit the undermining of none of our own which make for employment and maintained activities.

Every contemplation, it little matters in which direction one turns, magnifies the difficulty of tariff legislation, but the necessity of the revision is magnified with it. Doubtless we are justified in seeking a more flexible policy than we have provided heretofore. I hope a way will be found to make for flexibility and elasticity, so that rates may be adjusted to meet unusual and changing conditions which cannot be accurately anticipated. There are problems incident to unfair practices, and to exchanges which madness in money have made almost unsolvable. I know of no manner in which to effect this flexibility other than the extension of the powers of the Tariff Commission, so that it can adapt itself to a scientific and wholly just administration of the law.

I am not unmindful of the constitutional difficulties. These can be met by giving authority to the Chief Executive, who could proclaim additional duties to meet conditions which the Congress may designate.

At this point I must disavow any desire to enlarge the Executive's powers or add to the responsibility of the office. They are already too large. If there were any other plan I would prefer it.

The grant of authority to proclaim would necessarily bring the Tariff Commission into new and enlarged activities, because no Executive could discharge such a duty except upon the information acquired and recommendations made by this commission. But the plan is feasible, and the proper functioning of the board would give us a better administration of a defined policy than ever can be made possible by tariff duties prescribed without flexibility.

There is a manifest difference of opinion about the merits of American valuation. Many nations have adopted delivery valuation as the basis for collecting duties; that is, they take the cost of the imports delivered at the port of entry as the basis for levying duty. It is no radical departure, in view of varying conditions and the disordered state of money values, to provide for American valuation, but there cannot be ignored the danger of such a valuation, brought to the level of our own production costs, making our tariffs prohibitive. It might do so in many instances where imports ought to be encouraged. I believe Congress ought well consider the desirability of the only promising alternative, namely, a provision authorizing proclaimed American valuation, under prescribed conditions, on any given list of articles imported.

In this proposed flexibility, authorizing increases to meet conditions so likely to change, there should also be provision for decreases. A rate may be just today, and entirely out of proportion six months from today. If our tariffs are to be made equitable, and not necessarily burden our imports and hinder our trade abroad, frequent adjustment will be necessary for years to come. Knowing the impossibility of modification by act of Congress for any one or a score of lines without involving a long array of schedules, I think we shall go a long ways toward stabilization, if there is recognition of the Tariff Commission's fitness to recommend urgent changes by proclamation.

I am sure about public opinion favoring the early determination of our tariff policy. There have been reassuring signs of a business revival from the deep slump which all the world has been experiencing. Our unemployment, which gave us deep concern only a few weeks ago, has grown encouragingly less, and new assurances and renewed confidence will attend the congressional declaration that American industry will be held secure.

Much has been said about the protective policy for ourselves making it impossible for our debtors to discharge their obligations to us. This is a contention not now pressing for decision. If we must choose between a people in idleness pressing for the payment of indebtedness, or a people resuming the normal ways of employment and carrying the credit, let us choose the latter. Sometimes we appraise largest the human ill most vivid in our minds. We have been giving, and are giving now, of our influence and appeals to minimize the likelihood of war and throw off the crushing burdens of armament. It is all very earnest, with a national soul impelling. But a people unemployed, and gaunt with hunger, face a situation quite as disheartening as war, and our greater obligation today is to do the Government's part toward resuming productivity and promoting fortunate and remunerative employment.

Something more than tariff protection is required by American agriculture. To the farmer has come the earlier and the heavier burdens of readjustment. There is actual depression in our agricultural industry, while agricultural prosperity is absolutely essential to the general prosperity of the country.

Congress has sought very earnestly to provide relief. It has promptly given such temporary relief as has been possible, but the call is insistent for the permanent solution. It is inevitable that large crops lower the prices and short crops advance them. No legislation can cure that fundamental law. But there must be some economic solution for the excessive variation in returns for agricultural production.

It is rather shocking to be told, and to have the statement strongly supported, that 9,000,000 bales of cotton, raised on American plantations in a given year, will actually be worth more to the producers than 13,000,000 bales would have been. Equally shocking is the statement that 700,000,000 bushels of wheat, raised by American farmers, would bring them more money than a billion bushels. Yet these are not exaggerated statements. In a world where there are tens of millions who need food and clothing which they cannot get, such a condition is sure to indict the social system which makes it possible.

In the main the remedy lies in distribution and marketing. Every proper encouragement should be given to the cooperative marketing programs. These have proven very helpful to the cooperating communities in Europe. In Russia the cooperative community has become the recognized bulwark of law and order, and saved individualism from engulfment in social paralysis. Ultimately they will be accredited with the salvation of the Russian State.

There is the appeal for this experiment. Why not try it? No one challenges the right of the farmer to a larger share of the consumer's pay for his product, no one disputes that we cannot live without the farmer. He is justified in rebelling against the transportation cost. Given a fair return for his labor, he will have less occasion to appeal for financial aid; and given assurance that his labors shall not be in vain, we reassure all the people of a production sufficient to meet our National requirement and guard against disaster.

The base of the pyramid of civilization which rests upon the soil is shrinking through the drift of population from farm to city. For a generation we have been expressing more or less concern about this tendency. Economists have warned and statesmen have deplored. We thought for a time that modern conveniences and the more intimate contact would halt the movement, but it has gone steadily on. Perhaps only grim necessity will correct it, but we ought to find a less drastic remedy.

The existing scheme of adjusting freight rates has been favoring the basing points, until industries are attracted to some centers and repelled from others. A great volume of uneconomic and wasteful transportation has attended, and the cost increased accordingly. The grain-milling and meat-packing industries afford ample illustration, and the attending concentration is readily apparent. The menaces in concentration are not limited to the retarding influences on agriculture. Manifestly the conditions and terms of railway transportation ought not be permitted to increase this undesirable tendency. We have a just pride in our great cities, but we shall find a greater pride in the Nation, which has a larger distribution of its population into the country, where comparatively self-sufficient smaller communities may blend agricultural and manufacturing interests in harmonious helpfulness and enhanced good fortune. Such a movement contemplates no destruction of things wrought, of investments made, or wealth involved. It only looks to a general policy of transportation, of distributed industry, and of highway construction, to encourage the spread of our population and restore the proper balance between city and country. The problem may well have your earnest attention.

It has been perhaps the proudest claim of our American civilization that in dealing with human relationships it has constantly moved toward such justice in distributing the product of human energy that it has improved continuously the economic status of the mass of people. Ours has been a highly productive social organization. On the way up from the elemental stages of society we have eliminated slavery and serfdom and are now far on the way to the elimination of poverty.

Through the eradication of illiteracy and the diffusion of education mankind has reached a stage where we may fairly say that in the United States equality of opportunity has been attained, though all are not prepared to embrace it. There is, indeed, a too great divergence between the economic conditions of the most and the least favored classes in the community. But even that divergence has now come to the point where we bracket the very poor and the very rich together as the least fortunate classes. Our efforts may well be directed to improving the status of both.

While this set of problems is commonly comprehended under the general phrase "Capital and labor," it is really vastly broader. It is a question of social and economic organization. Labor has become a large contributor, through its savings, to the stock of capital; while the people who own the largest individual aggregates of capital are themselves often hard and earnest laborers. Very often it is extremely difficult to draw the line of demarcation between the two groups; to determine whether a particular individual is entitled to be set down as laborer or as capitalist. In a very large proportion of cases he is both, and when he is both he is the most useful citizen.

The right of labor to organize is just as fundamental and necessary as is the right of capital to organize. The right of labor to negotiate, to deal with and solve its particular problems in an organized way, through its chosen agents, is just as essential as is the right of capital to organize, to maintain corporations, to limit the liabilities of stockholders. Indeed, we have come to recognize that the limited liability of the citizen as a member of a labor organization closely parallels the limitation of liability of the citizen as a stockholder in a corporation for profit. Along this line of reasoning we shall make the greatest progress toward solution of our problem of capital and labor.

In the case of the corporation which enjoys the privilege of limited liability of stockholders, particularly when engaged in the public service, it is recognized that the outside public has a large concern which must be protected; and so we provide regulations, restrictions, and in some cases detailed supervision. Likewise in the case of labor organizations, we might well apply similar and equally well-defined principles of regulation and supervision in order to conserve the public's interests as affected by their operations.

Just as it is not desirable that a corporation shall be allowed to impose undue exactions upon the public, so it is not desirable that a labor organization shall be permitted to exact unfair terms of employment or subject the public to actual distresses in order to enforce its terms. Finally, just as we are earnestly seeking for procedures whereby to adjust and settle political differences between nations without resort to war, so we may well look about for means to settle the differences between organized capital and organized labor without resort to those forms of warfare which we recognize under the name of strikes, lockouts, boycotts, and the like.

As we have great bodies of law carefully regulating the organization and operations of industrial and financial corporations, as we have treaties and compacts among nations which look to the settlement of differences without the necessity of conflict in arms, so we might well have plans of conference, of common counsel, of mediation, arbitration, and judicial determination in controversies between labor and capital. To accomplish this would involve the necessity to develop a thoroughgoing code of practice in dealing with such affairs. It might be well to frankly set forth the superior interest of the community as a whole to either the labor group or the capital group. With rights, privileges, immunities, and modes of organization thus carefully defined, it should be possible to set up judicial or quasi judicial tribunals for the consideration and determination of all disputes which menace the public welfare.

In an industrial society such as ours the strike, the lockout, and the boycott are as much out of place and as disastrous in their results as is war or armed revolution in the domain of politics. The same disposition to reasonableness, to conciliation, to recognition of the other side's point of view, the same provision of fair and recognized tribunals and processes, ought to make it possible to solve the one set of questions as easily as the other. I believe the solution is possible.

The consideration of such a policy would necessitate the exercise of care and deliberation in the construction of a code and a charter of elemental rights, dealing with the relations of employer and employee. This foundation in the law, dealing with the modern conditions of social and economic life, would hasten the building of the temple of peace in industry which a rejoicing nation would acclaim.

After each war, until the last, the Government has been enabled to give homes to its returned soldiers, and a large part of our settlement and development has attended this generous provision of land for the Nation's defenders.

There is yet unreserved approximately 200,000,000 acres in the public domain, 20,000,000 acres of which are known to be susceptible of reclamation and made fit for homes by provision for irrigation.

The Government has been assisting in the development of its remaining lands, until the estimated increase in land values in the irrigated sections is full $500,000,000, and the crops of 1920 alone on these lands are estimated to exceed $100,000,000. Under the law authorizing these expenditures for development the advances are to be returned, and it would be good business for the Government to provide for the reclamation of the remaining 20,000,000 acres, in addition to expediting the completion of projects long under way.

Under what is known as the coal and gas lease law, applicable also to deposits of phosphates and other minerals on the public domain, leases are now being made on the royalty basis, and are producing large revenues to the Government. Under this legislation, 10 per centum of all royalties is to be paid directly to the Federal Treasury, and of the remainder 50 per centum is to be used for reclamation of arid lands by irrigation, and 40 per centum is to be paid to the States, in which the operations are located, to be used by them for school and road purposes.

These resources are so vast, and the development is affording so reliable a basis of estimate, that the Interior Department expresses the belief that ultimately the present law will add in royalties and payments to the treasuries of the Federal Government and the States containing these public lands a total of $12,000,000,000. This means, of course, an added wealth of many times that sum. These prospects seem to afford every justification of Government advances in reclamation and irrigation.

Contemplating the inevitable and desirable increase of population, there is another phase of reclamation full worthy of consideration. There are 79,000,000 acres of swamp and cut-over lands which may be reclaimed and made as valuable as any farm lands we possess. These acres are largely located in Southern States, and the greater proportion is owned by the States or by private citizens. Congress has a report of the survey of this field for reclamation, and the feasibility is established. I gladly commend Federal aid, by way of advances, where State and private participation is assured.

Home making is one of the greater benefits which government can bestow. Measures are pending embodying this sound policy to which we may well adhere. It is easily possible to make available permanent homes which will provide, in turn, for prosperous American families, without injurious competition with established activities, or imposition on wealth already acquired.

While we are thinking of promoting the fortunes of our own people I am sure there is room in the sympathetic thought of America for fellow human beings who are suffering and dying of starvation in Russia. A severe drought in the Valley of the Volga has plunged 15,000,000 people into grievous famine. Our voluntary agencies are exerting themselves to the utmost to save the lives of children in this area, but it is now evident that unless relief is afforded the loss of life will extend into many millions. America cannot be deaf to such a call as that.

We do not recognize the government of Russia, nor tolerate the propaganda which emanates therefrom, but we do not forget the traditions of Russian friendship. We may put aside our consideration of all international politics and fundamental differences in government. The big thing is the call of the suffering and the dying. Unreservedly I recommend the appropriation necessary to supply the American Relief Administration with 10,000,000 bushels of corn and 1,000,000 bushels of seed grains, not alone to halt the wave of death through starvation, but to enable spring planting in areas where the seed grains have been exhausted temporarily to stem starvation.

The American Relief Administration is directed in Russia by former officers of our own armies, and has fully demonstrated its ability to transport and distribute relief through American hands without hindrance or loss. The time has come to add the Government's support to the wonderful relief already wrought out of the generosity of the American private purse.

I am not unaware that we have suffering and privation at home. When it exceeds the capacity for the relief within the States concerned, it will have Federal consideration. It seems to me we should be indifferent to our own heart promptings, and out of accord with the spirit which acclaims the Christmastide, if we do not give out of our national abundance to lighten this burden of woe upon a people blameless and helpless in famine's peril.

There are a full score of topics concerning which it would be becoming to address you, and on which I hope to make report at a later time. I have alluded to the things requiring your earlier attention. However, I cannot end this limited address without a suggested amendment to the organic law.

Many of us belong to that school of thought which is hesitant about altering the fundamental law. I think our tax problems, the tendency of wealth to seek nontaxable investment, and the menacing increase of public debt, Federal, State and municipal—all justify a proposal to change the Constitution so as to end the issue of nontaxable bonds. No action can change the status of the many billions outstanding, but we can guard against future encouragement of capital's paralysis, while a halt in the grown of public indebtedness would be beneficial throughout our whole land.

Such a change in the Constitution must be very thoroughly considered before submission. There ought to be known what influence it will have on the inevitable refunding of our vast national debt, how it will operate on the necessary refunding of State and municipal debt, how the advantages of Nation over State and municipality, or the contrary, may be avoided. Clearly the States would not ratify to their own apparent disadvantage. I suggest the consideration because the drift of wealth into nontaxable securities is hindering the flow of large capital to our industries, manufacturing, agricultural, and carrying, until we are discouraging the very activities which make our wealth.

Agreeable to your expressed desire and in complete accord with the purposes of the executive branch of the Government, there is in Washington, as you happily know, an International Conference now most earnestly at work on plans for the limitation of armament, a naval holiday, and the just settlement of problems which might develop into causes of international disagreement.

It is easy to believe a world-hope is centered on this Capital City. A most gratifying world-accomplishment is not improbable.

FOUR-POWER PACT
December 13, 1921

Agreement was reached at the Washington Conference by the United States, France, Great Britain and Japan to respect each other's insular dominions in the Pacific area. It also terminated the Anglo-Japanese alliance. The treaty was declared in force on August 17, 1923.

The United States of America, the British Empire, France and Japan,

with a view to the preservation of the general peace and the maintenance of their rights in relation to their insular possessions and insular dominions in the region of the Pacific Ocean. . . .

I. The high contracting parties agree as between themselves to respect their rights in relation to their insular possessions and insular dominions in the region of the Pacific Ocean.

If there should develop between any of the high contracting parties a controversy arising out of any Pacific question and involving their said rights which is not satisfactorily settled by diplomacy and is likely to affect the harmonious accord now happily subsisting between them, they shall invite the other high contracting parties to a joint conference to which the whole subject will be referred for consideration and adjustment.

II. If the said rights are threatened by the aggressive action of any other power, the high contracting parties shall communicate with one another fully and frankly in order to arrive at an understanding as to the most efficient measures to be taken, jointly or separately, to meet the exigencies of the particular situation.

III. This treaty shall remain in force for 10 years from the time it shall take effect, and after the expiration of said period it shall continue to be in force subject to the right of any of the high contracting parties to terminate it upon 12 months' notice.

IV. This treaty shall be ratified as soon as possible in accordance with the constitutional methods of the high contracting parties and shall take effect on the deposit of ratifications, which shall take place at Washington, and thereupon the agreement between Great Britain and Japan, which was concluded at London on July 13, 1911, shall terminate. The government of the United States will transmit to all the signatory powers a certified copy . . . of ratifications. . . .

FIVE-POWER NAVAL TREATY
February 6, 1922

The treaty signed by the "big five" naval powers resulted in a 5:5:3 naval-strength ratio for the United States, Great Britain and Japan, and ratios of 1:75 for both France and Italy. The treaty was proclaimed in effect on August 21, 1923.

Treaty Between The United States, The British Empire, France, Italy, and Japan, Agreeing to a Limitation of Naval Armament.

The United States of America, the British Empire, France, Italy, and Japan:

Desiring to contribute to the maintenance of the general peace and to reduce the burdens of competition in armament:

Have resolved, with a view to accomplishing these purposes, to conclude a treaty to limit their respective naval armament, and to that end have appointed as their plenipotentiaries:

The President of the United States of America: Charles Evans Hughes, Henry Cabot Lodge, Oscar W. Underwood, Elihu Root, citizens of the United States;

His Majesty the King of the United Kingdom of Great Britain and Ireland and of the British Dominions beyond the Seas, Emperor of India: The Right Hon. Arthur James Balfour, O.M., M.P., Lord President of His Privy Council; the Right Hon. Baron Lee of Fareham, G.B.E., K.C.B., First Lord of His Admiralty; the Right Hon. Sir Auckland Campbell Geddes, K.C.B., His Ambassador Extraordinary and Plenipotentiary to the United States of America;

And for the Dominion of Canada: The Right Hon. Sir Robert Laird Borden, G.C.M.G., K.C.;

For the Commonwealth of Australia: Senator the Right Hon. George Foster Pearce, Minister for Home and Territories;

For the Dominion of New Zealand: The Hon. Sir John William Salmond, K.C., Judge of the Supreme Court of New Zealand;

For the Union of South Africa: The Right Hon. Arthur James Balfour, O.M., M.P.;

For India: The Right Hon. Valingman Sankaranarayana Srinivasa Sastri, Member of the Indian Council of State;

The President of the French Republic: Mr. Albert Sarraut, Deputy, Minister of the Colonies; Mr. Jules J. Jusserand, Ambassador Extraordinary and Plenipotentiary to the United States of America, Grand Cross of the National Order of the Legion of Honor;

His Majesty the King of Italy: The Hon. Carlo Schanzer, Senator of the

Kingdom; the Hon. Vittorio Rolandi Ricci, Senator of the Kingdom, His Ambassador Extraordinary and Plenipotentiary at Washington; the Hon. Luigi Albertini, Senator of the Kingdom;

His Majesty the Emperor of Japan: Baron Tomosaburo Kato, Minister for the Navy Junii, a member of the First Class of the Imperial Order of the Grand Cordon of the Rising Sun with the Paulownia Flower; Baron Kijuro Shidehara, His Ambassador Extraordinary and Plenipotentiary at Washington, Joshii, a member of the First Class of the Imperial Order of the Rising Sun; Mr. Masanao Hanihara, Vice Minister for Foreign Affairs, Jushii, a member of the Second Class of the Imperial Order of the Rising Sun;

Who, having communicated to each other their respective full powers, found to be in good and due form, have agreed as follows:

CHAPTER I
General provisions relating to the limitation of naval armament

Article I

The contracting powers agree to limit their respective naval armament as provided in the present treaty.

Article II

The contracting powers may retain, respectively, the capital ships which are specified in Chapter II, part 1. On the coming into force of the present treaty, but subject to the following provisions of this article, all other capital ships, built or building, of the United States, the British Empire, and Japan shall be disposed of as prescribed in Chapter II, part 2.

In addition to the capital ships specified in Chapter II, part 1, the United States may complete and retain two ships of the *West Virginia* class now under construction. On the completion of these two ships the *North Dakota* and *Delaware* shall be disposed of as prescribed in Chapter II, part 2.

The British Empire may, in accordance with the replacement table in Chapter II, part 3, construct two new capital ships not exceeding 35,000 tons (35,560 metric tons) standard displacement each. On the completion of the said two ships the *Thunderer*, *King George V*, *Ajax*, and *Centurion* shall be disposed of as prescribed in Chapter II, part 2.

Article III

Subject to the provisions of Article II, the contracting powers shall abandon their respective capital ship-building programs, and no new capital ships shall be constructed or acquired by any of the contracting powers except replacement tonnage which may be constructed or acquired as specified in Chapter II, part 3.

Ships which are replaced in accordance with Chapter II, part 3, shall be disposed of as prescribed in part 2 of that chapter.

Article IV

The total capital ship replacement tonnage of each of the contracting powers shall not exceed in standard displacement, for the United States, 525,000 tons (533,400 metric tons); for the British Empire, 525,000 tons (533,400 metric tons); for France, 175,000 tons (177,800 metric tons); for Italy, 175,000 tons (177,800 metric tons); for Japan, 315,000 tons (320,040 metric tons).

Article V

No capital ship exceeding 35,000 tons (35,560 metric tons) standard displacement shall be acquired by, or constructed by, for, or within the jurisdiction of, any of the contracting powers.

Article VI

No capital ship of any of the contracting powers shall carry a gun with a caliber in excess of 16 inches (406 millimeters).

Article VII

The total tonnage for aircraft carriers of each of the contracting powers shall not exceed in standard displacement, for the United States 135,000 tons (137,160 metric tons); for the British Empire 135,000 tons (137,160 metric tons); for France 60,000 tons (60,960 metric tons); for Italy 60,000 tons (60,960 metric tons); for Japan 81,000 tons (82,296 metric tons).

Article VIII

The replacement of aircraft carriers shall be effected only as prescribed in Chapter II, part 3, provided, however, that all aircraft carrier tonnage in existence or building on November 12, 1921, shall be considered experimental, and may be replaced, within the total tonnage limit prescribed in Article VII, without regard to its age.

Article IX

No aircraft carrier exceeding 27,000 tons (27,432 metric tons) standard displacement shall be acquired by, or constructed by, for, or within the jurisdiction of, any of the contracting powers.

However, any of the contracting powers may, provided that its total tonnage allowance of aircraft carriers is not thereby exceeded, build not more than two aircraft carriers, each of a tonnage of not more than 33,000 tons (33,528 metric tons) standard displacement, and in order to effect economy any of the contracting powers may use for this purpose any two of their ships, whether constructed or in course of construction, which would otherwise be scrapped under the provisions of Article II. The armament of any aircraft carriers exceeding 27,000 tons (27,432 metric tons) standard displacement shall be in accordance with the requirements of Article X, except that the total number of guns to be carried in case any of such guns be of a caliber exc   g 6 inches (152 millimeters), except antiaircraft guns and guns not exceeding 5 inches (127 millimeters), shall not exceed eight.

Article X

No aircraft carrier of any of the contracting powers shall carry a gun with a caliber in excess of 8 inches (203 millimeters). Without prejudice to the provisions of Article IX, if the armament carried includes guns exceeding 6 inches (152 millimeters) in caliber the total number of guns carried, except antiaircraft guns and guns not exceeding 5 inches (127 millimeters), shall not exceed 10. If alternatively the armament contains no guns exceeding 6 inches (152 millimeters) in caliber, the number of guns is not limited. In either case the number of antiaircraft guns and of guns not exceeding 5 inches (127 millimeters) is not limited.

Article XI

No vessel of war exceeding 10,000 tons (10,160 metric tons) standard displacement, other than a capital ship or aircraft carrier, shall be acquired by, or constructed by, for, or within the jurisdiction of, any of the contracting powers. Vessels not specifically built as fighting ships nor taken in time of peace under government control for fighting purposes, which are employed on fleet duties or as troop transports or in some other way for the purpose of assisting in the prosecution of hostilities otherwise than as fighting ships, shall not be within the limitations of this article.

Article XII

No vessel of war of any of the contracting powers hereafter laid down, other than a capital ship, shall carry a gun with a caliber in excess of 8 inches (203 millimeters).

Article XIII

Except as provided in Article IX, no ship designated in the present treaty to be scrapped may be reconverted into a vessel of war.

Article XIV

No preparations shall be made in merchant ships in time of peace for the installation of warlike armaments for the purpose of converting such ships into vessels of war, other than the necessary stiffening of decks for the mounting of guns not exceeding 6-inch (152 millimeters) caliber.

Article XV

No vessel of war constructed within the jurisdiction of any of the contracting powers for a noncontracting power shall exceed the limitations as to displacement and armament prescribed by the present treaty for vessels of a similar type which may be constructed by or for any of the contracting powers: *Provided, however,* That the displacement for aircraft carriers constructed for a noncontracting power shall in no case exceed 27,000 tons (27,432 metric tons) standard displacement.

Article XVI

If the construction of any vessel of war for a noncontracting power is undertaken within the jurisdiction of any of the contracting powers, such power shall promptly inform the other contracting powers of the date of the signing of the contract and the date on which the keel of the ship is laid; and shall also communicate to them the particulars relating to the ship prescribed in Chapter II, part 3, section 1 (b), (4) and (5).

Article XVII

In the event of a contracting power being engaged in war, such power shall not use as a vessel of war any vessel of war which may be under construction within its jurisdiction for any other power, or which may have been constructed within its jurisdiction for another power and not delivered.

Article XVIII

Each of the contracting powers undertakes not to dispose by gift, sale, or any mode of transfer of any vessel of war in such a manner that such vessel may become a vessel of war in the navy of any foreign power.

Article XIX

The United States, the British Empire, and Japan agree that the status quo at the time of the signing of the present treaty, with regard to fortifications and naval bases, shall be maintained in their respective territories and possessions specified hereunder:

(1) The insular possessions which the United States now holds or may hereafter acquire in the Pacific Ocean, except (a) those adjacent to the coast of the United States, Alaska, and the Panama Canal Zone, not including the Aleutian Islands, and (b) the Hawaiian Islands.

(2) Hongkong and the insular possessions which the British Empire now holds or may hereafter acquire in the Pacific Ocean, east of the meridian of 110° east longitude, except (a) those adjacent to the coast of Canada, (b) the Commonwealth of Australia and its territories, and (c) New Zealand.

(3) The following insular territories and possessions of Japan in the Pacific Ocean, to wit, the Kurile Islands, the Bonin Islands. Amami-Oshima, the Loochoo Islands, Formosa, and the Pescadores, and any insular territories or possessions in the Pacific Ocean which Japan may hereafter acquire.

The maintenance of the status quo under the foregoing provisions implies that no new fortifications or naval bases shall be established in the territories and possessions specified; that no measures shall be taken to increase the existing naval facilities for the repair and maintenance of naval forces, and that no increase shall be made in the coast defenses of the territories and possessions above specified. This restriction, however, does not preclude such repair and replacement of worn-out weapons and equipment as is customary in naval and military establishments in time of peace.

Article XX

The rules for determining tonnage displacement prescribed in Chapter II, part 4, shall apply to the ships of each of the contracting powers.

NINE-POWER TREATY
February 6, 1922

*An attempt was made at the Washington Conference to guarantee
the territorial integrity of China and to formally state the open door
policy. Proclaimed in effect on August 5, 1925, it was soon to be
violated by Japan.*

The United States of America, Belgium, the British Empire, China, France,
Italy, Japan, the Netherlands and Portugal:

Desiring to adopt a policy designed to stabilize conditions in the Far
East, to safeguard the rights and interests of China, and to promote
intercourse between China and the other Powers upon the basis of equality of
opportunity....

I. The Contracting Powers, other than China, agree:

(1) To respect the sovereignty, the independence, and the territorial and
administrative integrity of China;

(2) To provide the fullest and most unembarrassed opportunity to China to
develop and maintain for herself an effective and stable government;

(3) To use their influence for the purpose of effectually establishing and
maintaining the principle of equal opportunity for the commerce and
industry of all nations throughout the territory of China;

(4) To refrain from taking advantage of conditions in China in order to
seek special rights or privileges which would abridge the rights of subjects or
citizens of friendly States, and from countenancing action inimical to the
security of such States.

II. The Contracting Powers agree not to enter into any treaty, agreement,
arrangement, or understanding, either with one another, or, individually or
collectively, with any Power or Powers, which would infringe or impair the
principles stated in Article I.

III. With a view to applying more effectually the principles of the Open
Door or equality of opportunity in China for the trade and industry of all
nations, the Contracting Powers, other than China, agree that they will not
seek nor support their respective nationals, in seeking

(a) any arrangement which might purport to establish in favor of their
interests any general superiority of rights with respect to commercial or
economic development in any designated region of China.

(b) any such monopoly or preference as would deprive the nationals of any
other Power of the right of undertaking any legitimate trade or industry in
China, or of participating with the Chinese Government, or with any local
authority, in any category of public enterprise, or which by reason of its
scope, duration or geographical extent is calculated to frustrate the practical
application of the principle of equal opportunity.

It is understood that the foregoing stipulations of this Article are not to be so construed as to prohibit the acquisition of such properties or rights as may be necessary to the conduct of a particular commercial, industrial, or financial undertaking or to the encouragement of invention and research.

China undertakes to be guided by the principles stated in the foregoing stipulations of this Article in dealing with applications for economic rights and privileges from Governments and nationals of all foreign countries, whether parties to the present Treaty or not.

IV. The Contracting Powers agree not to support any agreements by their respective nationals with each other designed to create Spheres of Influence or to provide for the enjoyment of mutually exclusive opportunities in designated parts of Chinese territory.

V. China agrees that, throughout the whole of the railways in China, she will not exercise or permit unfair discrimination of any kind. In particular there shall be no discrimination whatever, direct or indirect, in respect of charges or of facilities on the ground of the nationality of passengers or the countries from which or to which they are proceeding, or the origin or ownership of goods or the country from which or to which they are consigned, or the nationality or ownership of the ship or other means of conveying such passengers or goods before or after their transport on the Chinese railways.

The Contracting Powers, other than China, assume a corresponding obligation in respect of any of the aforesaid railways over which they or their nationals are in a position to exercise any control in virtue of any concession, special agreement or otherwise.

VI. The Contracting Powers, other than China, agree fully to respect China's rights as a neutral in time of war to which China is not a party; and China declares that when she is a neutral she will observe the obligations of neutrality.

VII. The Contracting Powers agree that, whenever a situation arises which in the opinion of any one of them involves the application of the stipulations of the present Treaty, and renders desirable discussion of such application, there shall be full and frank communication between the Contracting Powers concerned.

VIII. Powers not signatory to the present Treaty, which have Governments recognized by the Signatory Powers and which have treaty relations with China, shall be invited to adhere to the present Treaty. To this end the Government of the United States will make the necessary communications to nonsignatory Powers and will inform the Contracting Powers of the replies received. Adherence by any Power shall become effective on receipt of notice thereof by the Government of the United States.

IX. The present Treaty shall be ratified by the Contracting Powers in accordance with their respective constitutional methods and shall take effect on the date of the deposit of all the ratifications, which shall take place at Washington as soon as possible. The Government of the United States will transmit to the other Contracting Powers a certified copy of the procès-verbal of the deposit of ratifications.

The present Treaty, of which the French and English texts are both authentic, shall remain deposited in the archives of the Government of the United States, and duly certified copies thereof shall be transmitted by that Government to the other Contracting Powers.

In faith whereof the above-named Plenipotentiaries have signed the Present Treaty.

Done at the City of Washington the sixth day of February One Thousand Nine Hundred and Twenty-Two.

TREATY WITH COLOMBIA
March 30, 1922

This treaty was designed to repay Colombia for losses incurred when President Roosevelt in 1903 encouraged the independence of the Republic of Panama to protect our interests in the Panama Canal. The treaty was signed April 6, 1914; approved with amendments by the Senate April 20, 1921; ratified by the President January 11, 1922; ratified by Colombia March 1, 1922, and proclaimed March 30.

Whereas a Treaty between the United States of America and the Republic of Colombia, for the settlement of their differences arising out of the events which took place on the Isthmus of Panama in November, 1903, was concluded by their respective Plenipotentiaries at Bogota on the sixth day of April in the year one thousand nine hundred and fourteen, which Treaty, in the English and Spanish languages, and as amended by the Senate of the United States, is word for word as follows:

Treaty

between the United States of America and the Republic of Colombia for the settlement of their differences arising out of the events which took place on the Isthmus of Panama in November 1903.

The United States of America and the Republic of Colombia, being desirous to remove all the misunderstandings growing out of the political events in Panama in November 1903; to restore the cordial friendship that formerly characterized the relations between the two countries, and also to define and regulate their rights and interests in respect of the interoceanic canal which the Government of the United States has constructed across the Isthmus of Panama, have resolved for this purpose to conclude a Treaty and have accordingly appointed as their Plenipotentiaries:

His Excellency the President of the United States of America, Thaddeus Austin Thomson, Envoy Extraordinary and Minister Plenipotentiary of the United States of America to the Government of the Republic of Colombia; and

His Excellency the President of the Republic of Colombia, Francisco Jose Urrutia, Minister for Foreign Affairs; Marco Fidel Suarez; First Designate to exercise the Executive Power; Nicolas Esguerra, Ex-Minister of State; Jose Maria Gonzalez Valencia, Senator; Rafael Uribe Uribe, Senator; and Antonio Jose Uribe, President of the House of Representatives;

Who, after communicating to each other their respective full powers, which were found to be in due and proper form, have agreed upon the following:

Article I

The Republic of Colombia shall enjoy the following rights in respect to the interoceanic Canal and the Panama Railway, the title to which is now vested entirely and absolutely in the United States of America, without any incumbrances or indemnities whatever.

1.—The Republic of Colombia shall be at liberty at all times to transport through the interoceanic Canal its troops, materials of war and ships of war, without paying any charges to the United States.

2.—The products of the soil and industry of Colombia passing through the Canal, as well as the Colombian mails, shall be exempt from any charge or duty other than those to which the products and mails of the United States may be subject. The products of the soil and industry of Colombia, such as cattle, salt and provisions, shall be admitted to entry in the Canal Zone, and likewise in the islands and main land occupied or which may be occupied by the United States as auxiliary and accessory thereto, without paying other duties or charges than those payable by similar products of the United States.

3.—Colombian citizens crossing the Canal Zone shall, upon production of proper proof of their nationality, be exempt from every toll, tax or duty to which citizens of the United States are not subject.

4.—Whenever traffic by the Canal is interrupted or whenever it shall be necessary for any other reason to use the railway, the troops, materials of war, products and mails of the Republic of Colombia, as above mentioned, shall, be transported on the Railway between Ancon and Cristobal or on any other Railway substituted therefor, paying only the same charges and duties as are imposed upon the troops, materials of war, products and mails of the United States. The officers, agents and employees of the Government of Colombia shall, upon production of proper proof of their official character or their employment, also be entitled to passage on the said Railway on the same terms as officers, agents and employees of the Government of the United States.

5.—Coal, petroleum and sea salt, being the products of Colombia, for Colombian consumption passing from the Atlantic coast of Colombia to any Colombian port on the Pacific coast, and vice-versa, shall, whenever traffic by the canal is interrupted, be transported over the aforesaid Railway free of any charge except the actual cost of handling and transportation, which shall not in any case exceed one half of the ordinary freight charges levied upon similar products of the United States passing over the Railway and in transit from one port to another of the United States.

Article II

The Government of the United States of America agrees to pay at the City of Washington to the Republic of Colombia the sum of twenty-five million dollars, gold, United States money, as follows: The sum of five million dollars shall be paid within six months after the exchange of ratifications of the present treaty, and reckoning from the date of that payment, the remaining twenty million dollars shall be paid in four annual installments of five million dollars each.

Article III

The Republic of Colombia recognizes Panama as an independent nation and taking as a basis the Colombian Law of June 9, 1855, agrees that the boundary shall be the following: From cape Tiburon to the headwaters of the Rio de la Miel and following the mountain chain by the ridge of Gandi to the Sierra de Chugargun and that of Mali going down by the ridges of Nigue to the heights of Aspave and from thence to a point on the Pacific half way between Cocalito and La Ardita.

In consideration of this recognition, the Government of the United States will, immediately after the exchange of the ratifications of the present Treaty, take the necessary steps in order to obtain from the Government of Panama the despatch of a duly accredited agent to negotiate and conclude with the Government of Colombia a Treaty of Peace and Friendship, with a view to bring about both the establishment of regular diplomatic relations between Colombia and Panama and the adjustment of all questions of pecuniary liability as between the two countries, in accordance with recognized principles of law and precedents.

Article IV

The present Treaty shall be approved and ratified by the High Contracting Parties in conformity with their respective laws, and the ratifications thereof shall be exchanged in the city of Bogota, as soon as may be possible.

In faith whereof, the said Plenipotentiaries have signed the present Treaty in duplicate and have hereunto affixed their respective seals.

##########

Done at the city of Bogota, the sixth day of April in the year of our Lord nineteen hundred and fourteen.

[seal] Thaddeus Austin Thomson
[seal] Francisco Jose Urrutia
[seal] Marco Fidel Suarez
[seal] Nicolas Esguerra
[seal] Jose M. Gonzalez Valencia
[seal] Rafael Uribe Uribe
[seal] Antonio Jose Uribe

And whereas the advice and consent of the Senate of the United States to the ratification of the said Treaty was given also with the "understanding, to be made a part of such treaty and ratification, that the provisions of section 1 of the treaty granting to the Republic of Colombia free passage through the Panama Canal for its troops, materials of war and ships of war, shall not apply in case of war between the Republic of Colombia and any other country";

And whereas the said Treaty as amended by the Senate and the above recited understanding of the Senate made a part of such Treaty have been duly ratified on both parts, and the ratifications of the two Governments were exchanged at Bogota on the first day of March, one thousand nine hundred and twenty-two;

Now, therefore, be it known that I, Warren G. Harding, President of the United States of America, have caused the said Treaty, as amended, and the said understanding, made a part thereof, to be made public, to the end that the same and every article and clause thereof may be observed and fulfilled with good faith by the United States and the citizens thereof.

In Testimony whereof, I have hereunto set my hand and caused the seal of the United States to be affixed.

Done at the city of Washington, this thirtieth day of March, in the year of our Lord one thousand nine hundred and twenty-two, and of the independence of the United States of America the one hundred and forty-sixth.

Warren G. Harding

By the President:
   Charles E. Hughes
     Secretary of State

SECOND ANNUAL MESSAGE
December 8, 1922

This was Harding's second and final message to Congress. His emphasis upon transportation is a reflection of the turmoil attending the railway strikes of 1922 and, no doubt, of his efforts to get Congress to adopt legislation aiding the merchant marine.

Members of the Congress:

So many problems are calling for solution that a recital of all of them, in the face of the known limitations of a short session of Congress, would seem to lack sincerity of purpose. It is four years since the World War ended, but the inevitable readjustment of the social and economic order is not more than barely begun. There is no acceptance of pre-war conditions anywhere in the world. In a very general way humanity harbors individual wishes to go on with war-time compensations for production, with pre-war requirements in expenditure. In short, everyone, speaking broadly, craves readjustment for everybody except himself, while there can be no just and permanent readjustment except when all participate.

The civilization which measured its strength of genius and the power of science and the resources of industries, in addition to testing the limits of man power and the endurance and heroism of men and women—that same civilization is brought to its severest test in restoring a tranquil order and committing humanity to the stable ways of peace.

If the sober and deliberate appraisal of pre-war civilization makes it seem a worthwhile inheritance, then with patience and good courage it will be preserved. There never again will be precisely the old order; indeed, I know of no one who thinks it to be desirable. For out of the old order came the war itself, and the new order, established and made secure, never will permit its recurrence.

It is no figure of speech to say we have come to the test of our civilization. The world has been passing—is today passing—through a great crisis. The conduct of war itself is not more difficult than the solution of the problems which necessarily follow. I am not speaking at this moment of the problem in its wider aspect of world rehabilitation or of international relationships. The reference is to our own social, financial, and economic problems at home. These things are not to be considered solely as problems apart from all international relationship, but every nation must be able to carry on for itself, else its international relationship will have scant importance.

Doubtless our own people have emerged from the World War tumult less impaired than most belligerent powers; probably we have made larger progress toward reconstruction. Surely we have been fortunate in diminishing unemployment, and our industrial and business activities, which are the lifeblood of our material existence, have been restored as in no other reconstruction period of like length in the history of the world. Had we escaped the coal and railway strikes, which had no excuse for their beginning and less justification for their delayed settlement, we should have done infinitely better. But labor was insistent on holding to the war heights, and heedless forces of reaction sought the pre-war levels, and both were wrong. In the folly of conflict our progress was hindered, and the heavy cost has not yet been fully estimated. There can be neither adjustment nor the penalty of the failure to readjust in which all do not somehow participate.

The railway strike accentuated the difficulty of the American farmer. The first distress of readjustment came to the farmer, and it will not be a readjustment fit to abide until he is relieved. The distress brought to the farmer does not affect him alone. Agricultural ill fortune is a national ill fortune. That one-fourth of our population which produces the food of the Republic and adds so largely to our export commerce must participate in the good fortunes of the Nation, else there is none worth retaining.

Agriculture is a vital activity in our national life. In it we had our beginning, and its westward march with the star of the empire has reflected the growth of the Republic. It has its vicissitudes which no legislation will prevent, its hardships for which no law can provide escape. But the Congress can make available to the farmer the financial facilities which have been built up under Government aid and supervision for other commercial and industrial enterprises. It may be done on the same solid fundamentals and make the vitally important agricultural industry more secure, and it must be done.

This Congress already has taken cognizance of the misfortune which precipitate deflation brought to American agriculture. Your measures of relief and the reduction of the Federal reserve discount rate undoubtedly saved the country from widespread disaster. The very proof of helpfulness already given is the strongest argument for the permanent establishment of widened credits, heretofore temporarily extended through the War Finance Corporation.

The Farm Loan Bureau, which already has proven its usefulness through the Federal land banks, may well have its powers enlarged to provide ample farm production credits as well as enlarged land credits. It is entirely practical to create a division in the Federal land banks to deal with production credits, with the limitations of time so adjusted to the farm turnover as the Federal reserve system provides for the turnover in the manufacturing and mercantile world. Special provision must be made for live-stock production credits, and the limit of land loans may be safely enlarged. Various measures are pending before you, and the best judgment of Congress ought to be expressed in a prompt enactment at the present session.

But American agriculture needs more than added credit facilities. The credits will help to solve the pressing problems growing out of war-inflated land values and the drastic deflation of three years ago, but permanent and deserved agricultural good fortune depends on better and cheaper transportation.

Here is an outstanding problem, demanding the most rigorous consideration of the Congress and the country. It has to do with more than agriculture. It provides the channel for the flow of the country's commerce. But the farmer is particularly hard hit. His market, so affected by the world consumption, does not admit of the price adjustment to meet carrying charges. In the last half of the year now closing the railways, broken in carrying capacity because of motive power and rolling stock out of order, though insistently declaring to the contrary, embargoed his shipments or denied him cars when fortunate markets were calling. Too frequently transportation failed while perishable products were turning from possible profit to losses counted in tens of millions.

I know of no problem exceeding in importance this one of transportation. In our complex and interdependent modern life transportation is essential to our very existence. Let us pass for the moment the menace in the possible paralysis of such service as we have and note the failure, for whatever reason, to expand our transportation to meet the Nation's needs.

The census of 1880 recorded a population of 50,000,000. In two decades more we may reasonably expect to count thrice that number. In the three decades ending in 1920 the country's freight by rail increased from 631,000,000 tons to 2,234,000,000 tons; that is to say, while our population was increasing less than 70 per cent, the freight movement increased over 250 per cent.

We have built 40 per cent of the world's railroad mileage, and yet find it inadequate to our present requirements. When we contemplate the inadequacy of today it is easy to believe that the next few decades will witness the paralysis of our transportation-using social scheme or a complete reorganization on some new basis. Mindful of the tremendous costs of betterments, extensions, and expansions, and mindful of the staggering debts of the world today, the difficulty is magnified. Here is a problem demanding wide vision and the avoidance of mere makeshifts. No matter what the errors of the past, no matter how we acclaimed construction and then condemned operations in the past, we have the transportation and the honest investment in the transportation which sped us on to what we are, and we face conditions which reflect its inadequacy today, its greater inadequacy tomorrow, and we contemplate transportation costs which much of the traffic cannot and will not continue to pay.

Manifestly, we have need to begin on plans to coordinate all transportation facilities. We should more effectively connect up our rail lines with our carriers by sea. We ought to reap some benefit from the hundreds of millions expended on inland waterways, proving our capacity to utilize as well as expend. We ought to turn the motor truck into a railway feeder and distributor instead of a destroying competitor.

It would be folly to ignore that we live in a motor age. The motor car reflects our standard of living and gauges the speed of our present-day life. It long ago ran down Simple Living, and never halted to inquire about the prostrate figure which fell as its victim. With full recognition of motor-car transportation we must turn it to the most practical use. It cannot supersede the railway lines, no matter how generously we afford it highways out of the Public Treasury. If freight traffic by motor were charged with its proper and proportionate share of highway construction, we should find much of it wasteful and more costly than like service by rail. Yet we have paralleled the railways, a most natural line of construction, and thereby taken away from the agency of expected service much of its profitable traffic, which the taxpayers have been providing the highways, whose cost of maintenance is not yet realized.

The Federal Government has a right to inquire into the wisdom of this policy, because the National Treasury is contributing largely to this highway construction. Costly highways ought to be made to serve as feeders rather than competitors of the railroads, and the motor truck should become a coordinate factor in our great distributing system.

This transportation problem cannot be waived aside. The demand for lowered costs on farm products and basic materials cannot be ignored. Rates horizontally increased, to meet increased wage outlays during the war inflation, are not easily reduced. When some very moderate wage reductions were effected last summer there was a 5 per cent horizontal reduction in rates. I sought at that time, in a very informal way, to have the railway managers go before the Interstate Commerce Commission and agree to a heavier reduction on farm products and coal and other basic commodities, and leave unchanged the freight tariffs which a very large portion of the traffic was able to bear. Neither the managers nor the commission saw fit to adopt the suggestion, so we had the horizontal reduction too slight to be felt by the higher class cargoes and too little to benefit the heavy tonnage calling most loudly for relief.

Railways are not to be expected to render the most essential service in our social organization without a fair return on capital invested, but the Government has gone so far in the regulation of rates and rules of operation that it has the responsibility of pointing the way to the reduced freight costs so essential to our national welfare.

Government operation does not afford the cure. It was Government operation which brought us to the very order of things against which we now rebel, and we are still liquidating the costs of that supreme folly.

Surely the genius of the railway builders has not become extinct among the railway managers. New economies, new efficiencies in cooperation must be found. The fact that labor takes 50 to 60 per cent of total railway earnings makes limitations within which to effect economies very difficult, but the demand is no less insistent on that account.

Clearly the managers are without that intercarrier, cooperative relationship so highly essential to the best and most economical operation. They could not function in harmony when the strike threatened the paralysis of all railway transportation. The relationship of the service to public welfare, so intimately affected by State and Federal regulation, demands the effective correlation and a concerted drive to meet an insistent and justified public demand.

The merger of lines into systems, a facilitated interchange of freight cars, the economic use of terminals, and the consolidation of facilities are suggested ways of economy and efficiency.

I remind you that Congress provided a Joint Commission of Agricultural Inquiry which made an exhaustive investigation of car service and transportation, and unanimously recommended in its report of October 15, 1921, the pooling of freight cars under a central agency. This report well deserves your serious consideration. I think well of the central agency, which shall be a creation of the railways themselves, to provide, under the jurisdiction of the Interstate Commerce Commission, the means for financing equipment for carriers which are otherwise unable to provide their proportion of car equipment adequate to transportation needs. This same agency ought to point the way to every possible economy in maintained equipment and the necessary interchanges in railway commerce.

In a previous address to the Congress I called to your attention the insufficiency of power to enforce the decisions of the Railroad Labor Board. Carriers have ignored its decisions, on the one hand, railway workmen have challenged its decisions by a strike, on the other hand.

The intent of Congress to establish a tribunal to which railway labor and managers may appeal respecting questions of wages and working conditions cannot be too strongly commended. It is vitally important that some such agency should be a guaranty against suspended operation. The public must be spared even the threat of discontinued service.

Sponsoring the railroads as we do, it is an obligation that labor shall be assured the highest justice and every proper consideration of wage and working conditions, but it is an equal obligation to see that no concerted action in forcing demands shall deprive the public of the transportation service essential to its very existence. It is now impossible to safeguard public interest, because the decrees of the board are unenforceable against either employer or employee.

The Labor Board itself is not so constituted as best to serve the public interest. With six partisan members on a board of nine, three partisans nominated by the employees and three by the railway managers, it is inevitable that the partisan viewpoint is maintained throughout hearings and in decisions handed down. Indeed, the few exceptions to a strictly partisan expression in decisions thus far rendered have been followed by accusations of betrayal of the partisan interests represented. Only the public group of three is free to function in unbiased decisions. Therefore the partisan membership may well be abolished, and decisions should be made by an impartial tribunal.

I am well convinced that the functions of this tribunal could be much better carried on here in Washington. Even were it to be continued as a separate tribunal, there ought to be contact with the Interstate Commerce Commission, which has supreme authority in the rate making to which wage cost bears an indissoluble relationship. Theoretically, a fair and living wage must be determined quite apart from the employer's earning capacity, but in practice, in the railway service, they are inseparable. The record of advanced rates to meet increased wages, both determined by the Government, is proof enough.

The substitution of a labor division in the Interstate Commerce Commission, made up from its membership, to hear and decide disputes relating to wages and working conditions which have failed of adjustment by proper committees created by the railways and their employees, offers a more effective plan.

It need not be surprising that there is dissatisfaction over delayed hearings and decisions by the present board when every trivial dispute is carried to that tribunal. The law should require the railroads and their employees to institute means and methods to negotiate between themselves their constantly arising differences, limiting appeals to the Government tribunal to disputes of such character as are likely to affect the public welfare.

This suggested substitution will involve a necessary increase in the membership of the commission, probably four, to constitute the labor division. If the suggestion appeals to the Congress, it will be well to specify that the labor division shall be constituted of representatives of the four rate-making territories, thereby assuring a tribunal conversant with the conditions which obtain in the different rate-making sections of the country.

I wish I could bring to you the precise recommendation for the prevention of strikes which threaten the welfare of the people and menace public safety. It is an impotent civilization and an inadequate government which lacks the genius and the courage to guard against such a menace to public welfare as we experienced last summer. You were aware of the Government's great concern and its futile attempt to aid in an adjustment. It will reveal the inexcusable obstinacy which was responsible for so much distress to the country to recall now that, though all disputes are not yet adjusted, the many settlements which have been made were on the terms which the Government proposed in mediation.

Public interest demands that ample power shall be conferred upon the labor tribunal, whether it is the present board or the suggested substitute, to require its rulings to be accepted by both parties to a disputed question.

Let there be no confusion about the purpose of the suggested conferment of power to make decisions effective. There can be no denial of constitutional rights of either railway workmen or railway managers. No man can be denied his right to labor when and how he chooses, or cease to labor when he so elects, but, since the Government assumes to safeguard his interests while employed in an essential public service, the security of society itself demands his retirement from the service shall not be so timed and related as to effect the destruction of that service. This vitally essential public transportation service, demanding so much of brain and brawn, so much for efficiency and security, ought to offer the most attractive working conditions and the highest of wages paid to workmen in any employment.

In essentially every branch, from track repairer to the man at the locomotive throttle, the railroad worker is responsible for the safety of human lives and the care of vast property. His high responsibility might well rate high his pay within the limits the traffic will bear; but the same responsibility, plus governmental protection, may justly deny him and his associates a withdrawal from service without a warning or under circumstances which involve the paralysis of necessary transportation. We have assumed so great a responsibility in necessary regulation that we unconsciously have assumed the responsibility for maintained service; therefore the lawful power for the enforcement of decisions is necessary to sustain the majesty of government and to administer to the public welfare.

During its longer session the present Congress enacted a new tariff law. The protection of the American standards of living demanded the insurance it provides against the distorted conditions of world commerce. The framers of the law made provision for a certain flexibility of customs duties, whereby it is possible to readjust them as developing conditions may require. The enactment has imposed a large responsibility upon the Executive, but that responsibility will be discharged with a broad mindfulness of the whole business situation. The provision itself admits either the possible fallibility of rates or their unsuitableness to changing conditions. I believe the grant of authority may be promptly and discreetly exercised, ever mindful of the intent and purpose to safeguard American industrial activity, and at the same time prevent the exploitation of the American consumer and keep open the paths of such liberal exchanges as do not endanger our own productivity.

No one contemplates commercial aloofness nor any other aloofness contradictory to the best American traditions or loftiest human purposes. Our fortunate capacity for comparative self-containment affords the firm foundation on which to build for our own security, and a like foundation on which to build for a future of influence and importance in world commerce.

Our trade expansion must come of capacity and of policies of righteousness and reasonableness in all our commercial relations.

Let no one assume that our provision for maintained good fortune at home, and our unwillingness to assume the correction of all the ills of the world, means a reluctance to cooperate with other peoples or to assume every just obligation to promote human advancement anywhere in the world.

War made us a creditor Nation. We did not seek an excess possession of the world's gold, and we have neither desire to profit unduly by its possession nor permanently retain it. We do not seek to become an international dictator because of its power.

The voice of the United States has a respectful hearing in international councils, because we have convinced the world that we have no selfish ends to serve, no old grievances to avenge, no territorial or other greed to satisfy. But the voice being heard is that of good counsel, not of dictation. It is the voice of sympathy and fraternity and helpfulness, seeking to assist but not assume for the United States burdens which nations must bear for themselves. We would rejoice to help rehabilitate currency systems and facilitate all commerce which does not drag us to the very levels of those we seek to lift up.

While I have everlasting faith in our Republic, it would be folly, indeed, to blind ourselves to our problems at home. Abusing the hospitality of our shores are the advocates of revolution, finding their deluded followers among those who take on the habiliments of an American without knowing an American soul. There is the recrudescence of hyphenated Americanism which we thought to have been stamped out when we committed the Nation, life and soul, to the World War.

There is a call to make the alien respect our institutions while he accepts our hospitality. There is need to magnify the American viewpoint to the alien who seeks a citizenship among us. There is need to magnify the national viewpoint to Americans throughout the land. More, there is a demand for every living being in the United States to respect and abide by the laws of the Republic. Let men who are rending the moral fiber of the Republic through easy contempt for the prohibition law, because they think it restricts their personal liberty, remember that they set the example and breed a contempt for law which will ultimately destroy the Republic.

Constitutional prohibition has been adopted by the Nation. It is the supreme law of the land. In plain speaking, there are conditions relating to its enforcement which savor of nationwide scandal. It is the most demoralizing factor in our public life.

Most of our people assumed that the adoption of the eighteenth amendment meant the elimination of the question from our politics. On the contrary, it has been so intensified as an issue that many voters are disposed to make all political decisions with reference to this single question. It is distracting the public mind and prejudicing the judgment of the electorate.

The day is unlikely to come when the eighteenth amendment will be repealed. The fact may as well be recognized and our course adapted accordingly. If the statutory provisions for its enforcement are contrary to deliberate public opinion, which I do not believe, the rigorous and literal enforcement will concentrate public attention on any requisite modification. Such a course conforms with the law and saves the humiliation of the Government and the humiliation of our people before the world, and challenges the destructive forces engaged in widespread violation, official corruption, and individual demoralization.

The eighteenth amendment involves the concurrent authority of State and Federal Governments for the enforcement of the policy it defines. A certain lack of definiteness, through division of responsibility, is thus introduced. I order to bring about a full understanding of duties and responsibilities as thus distributed, I purpose to invite the governors of the States and Territories, at an early opportunity, to a conference with the Federal Executive authority. Out of the full and free considerations which will thus be possible, it is confidently believed, will emerge a more adequate comprehension of the whole problem, and definite policies of National and State cooperation in administering the laws.

There are pending bills for the registration of the alien who has come to our shores. I wish the passage of such an act might be expedited. Life amid American opportunities is worth the cost of registration if it is worth the seeking, and the Nation has the right to know who are citizens in the making or who live among us and share our advantages while seeking to undermine our cherished institutions. This provision will enable us to guard against the abuses in immigration, checking the undesirable whose irregular coming is his first violation of our laws. More, it will facilitate the needed Americanizing of those who mean to enroll as fellow citizens.

Before enlarging the immigration quotas we had better provide registration for aliens, those now here or continually pressing for admission, and establish our examination boards abroad, to make sure of desirables only. By the examination abroad we could end the pathos at our ports, when men and women find our doors closed, after long voyages and wasted savings, because they are unfit for admission. It would be kindlier and safer to tell them before they embark.

Our program of admission and treatment of immigrants is very intimately related to the educational policy of the Republic. With illiteracy estimated at from two-tenths of 1 per cent to less than 2 per cent in 10 of the foremost nations of Europe, it rivets our attention to a serious problem when we are reminded of a 6 per cent illiteracy in the United States. The figures are based on the test which defines an illiterate as one having no schooling whatever. Remembering the wide freedom of our public schools, with compulsory attendance in many States in the Union, one is convinced that much of our excessive illiteracy comes to us from abroad, and the education of the immigrant becomes a requisite to his Americanization. It must be done if he is fittingly to exercise the duties as well as enjoy the privileges of American citizenship. Here is revealed the special field for Federal cooperation in furthering education.

From the very beginning public education has been left mainly in the hands of the States. So far as schooling youth is concerned the policy has been justified, because no responsibility can be so effective as that of the local community alive to its task. I believe in the cooperation of the national authority to stimulate, encourage, and broaden the work of the local authorities. But it is the especial obligation of the Federal Government to devise means and effectively assist in the education of the newcomer from foreign lands, so that the level of American education may be made the highest that is humanly possible.

Closely related to this problem of education is the abolition of child labor. Twice Congress has attempted the correction of the evils incident to child employment. The decision of the Supreme Court has put this problem outside the proper domain of Federal regulation until the Constitution is so amended as to give the Congress indubitable authority. I recommend the submission of such an amendment.

We have two schools of thought relating to amendment of the Constitution. One need not be committed to the belief that amendment is weakening the fundamental law, or that excessive amendment is essential to meet every ephemeral whim. We ought to amend to meet the demands of the people when sanctioned by deliberate public opinion.

One year ago I suggested the submission of an amendment so that we may lawfully restrict the issues of tax-exempt securities, and I renew that recommendation now. Tax-exempt securities are drying up the sources of Federal taxation and they are encouraging unproductive and extravagant expenditures by States and municipalities. There is more than the menace in mounting public debt, there is the dissipation of capital which should be made available to the needs of productive industry. The proposed amendment will place the State and Federal Governments and all political subdivisions on an exact equality, and will correct the growing menace of public borrowing, which if left unchecked may soon threaten the stability of our institutions.

We are so vast and so varied in our national interests that scores of problems are pressing for attention. I must not risk the wearying of your patience with detailed reference.

Reclamation and irrigation projects, where waste land may be made available for settlement and productivity, are worthy of your favorable consideration.

When it is realized that we are consuming our timber four times as rapidly as we are growing it, we must encourage the greatest possible cooperation between the Federal Government, the various States, and the owners of forest lands, to the end that protection from fire shall be made more effective and replanting encouraged.

The fuel problem is under study now by a very capable fact-finding commission, and any attempt to deal with the coal problem, of such deep concern to the entire Nation, must await the report of the commission.

There are necessary studies of great problems which Congress might well initiate. The wide spread between production costs and prices which consumers pay concerns every citizen of the Republic. It contributes very largely to the unrest in agriculture and must stand sponsor for much against which we inveigh in that familiar term—the high cost of living.

No one doubts the excess is traceable to the levy of the middleman, but it would be unfair to charge him with all responsibility before we appraise what is exacted of him by our modernly complex life. We have attacked the problem on one side by the promotion of cooperative marketing, and we might well inquire into the benefits of cooperative buying. Admittedly, the consumer is much to blame himself, because of his prodigal expenditure and his exaction of service, but Government might well serve to point the way of narrowing the spread of price, especially between the production of food and its consumption.

A superpower survey of the eastern industrial region has recently been completed, looking to unification of steam, water, and electric powers, and to a unified scheme of power distribution. The survey proved that vast economies in tonnage movement of freights, and in the efficiency of the railroads, would be effected if the superpower program were adopted. I am convinced that constructive measures calculated to promote such an industrial development—I am tempted to say, such an industrial revolution—would be well worthy the careful attention and fostering interest of the National Government.

The proposed survey of a plan to draft all the resources of the Republic, human and material, for national defense may well have your approval. I commended such a program in case of future war, in the inaugural address of March 4, 1921, and every experience in the adjustment and liquidation of war claims and the settlement of war obligations persuades me we ought to be prepared for such universal call to armed defense.

I bring you no apprehension of war. The world is abhorrent of it, and our own relations are not only free from every threatening cloud, but we have contributed our larger influence toward making armed conflict less likely.

Those who assume that we played our part in the World War and later took ourselves aloof and apart, unmindful of world obligations, give scant credit to the helpful part we assume in international relationships.

Whether all nations signatory ratify all the treaties growing out of the

Washington Conference on Limitation of Armament or some withhold approval, the underlying policy of limiting naval armament has the sanction of the larger naval powers, and naval competition is suspended. Of course, unanimous ratification is much to be desired.

The four-power pact, which abolishes every probability of war on the Pacific, has brought new confidence in a maintained peace, and I can well believe it might be made a model for like assurances wherever in the world any common interests are concerned.

We have had expressed the hostility of the American people to a supergovernment or to any commitment where either a council or an assembly of leagued powers may chart our course. Treaties of armed alliance can have no likelihood of American sanction, but we believe in respecting the rights of nations, in the value of conference and consultation, in the effectiveness of leaders of nations looking each other in the face before resorting to the arbitrament of arms.

It has been our fortune both to preach and promote international understanding. The influence of the United States in bringing near the settlement of an ancient dispute between South American nations is added proof of the glow of peace in ample understanding. In Washington today are met the delegates of the Central American nations, gathered at the table of international understanding, to stabilize their Republics and remove every vestige of disagreement. They are met here by our invitation, not in our aloofness, and they accept our hospitality because they have faith in our unselfishness and believe in our helpfulness. Perhaps we are selfish in craving their confidence and friendship, but such a selfishness we proclaim to the world, regardless of hemisphere, or seas dividing.

I would like the Congress and the people of the Nation to believe that in a firm and considerate way we are insistent on American rights wherever they may be questioned, and deny no rights of others in the assertion of our own. Moreover we are cognizant of the world's struggles for full readjustment and rehabilitation, and we have shirked no duty which comes of sympathy, or fraternity, or highest fellowship among nations. Every obligation consonant with American ideals and sanctioned under our form of government is willingly met. When we cannot support we do not demand. Our constitutional limitations do not forbid the exercise of a moral influence, the measure of which is not less than the high purposes we have sought to serve.

After all there is less difference about the part this great Republic shall play in furthering peace and advancing humanity than in the manner of playing it. We ask no one to assume responsibility for us; we assume no responsibility which others must bear for themselves, unless nationality is hopelessly swallowed up in internationalism.

FORDNEY-McCUMBER ACT
September 21, 1922

By this act, Congress established the highest tariffs in the nation's history to protect the American producer. This brief excerpt indicates the comprehensiveness of the imposts.

TITLE I
Dutiable List

Section 1. That on and after the day following the passage of this Act, except as otherwise specially provided for in this Act, there shall be levied, collected, and paid upon all articles when imported from any foreign country into the United States or into any of its possessions (except the Philippine Islands, the Virgin Islands, and the islands of Guam and Tutuila) the rates of duty which are prescribed by the schedules and paragraphs of the dutiable list of this title, namely:

Schedule 1—Chemicals, Oils, and Paints

Paragraph 1. Acids and acid anhydrides: Acetic acid containing by weight not more than 65 per centum of acetic acid, three-fourths of 1 cent per pound; containing by weight more than 65 per centum, 2 cents per pound; acetic anhydride, 5 cents per pound; boric acid, 1½ cents per pound; chloroacetic acid, 5 cents per pound; citric acid, 17 cents per pound; lactic acid, containing by weight of lactic acid less than 30 per centum, 2 cents per pound; 30 per centum or more and less than 55 per centum, 4 cents per pound; and 55 per centum or more, 9 cents per pound: *Provided,* That any lactic-acid anhydride present shall be determined as lactic acid and included as such: *And provided further,* That the duty on lactic acid shall not be less than 25 per centum ad valorem; tannic acid, tannin, and extracts of nutgalls, containing by weight of tannic acid less than 50 per centum, 4 cents per pound; 50 per centum or more and not medicinal, 10 cents per pound; 50 per centum or more and medicinal, 20 cents per pound; tartaric acid, 6 cents per pound; arsenic acid, 3 cents per pound; gallic acid, 8 cents per pound; oleic acid or red oil, 1½ cents per pound; oxalic acid, 4 cents per pound; phosphoric acid, 2 cents per pound; pyrogallic acid, 12 cents per pound; stearic acid, 1½ cents per pound; and all other acids and acid anhydrides not specially provided for, 25 per centum ad valorem.

Par. 2. Acetaldehyde, aldol or acetaldol, aldehyde ammonia, butyr-aldehyde, crotonaldehyde, paracetaldehyde, ethylene chlorohydrin, ethylene dichloride, ethylene glycol, ethylene oxide, glycol monoacetate, propylene chlorohydrin, propylene dichloride, and propylene glycol, 6 cents per pound and 30 per centum ad valorem.

Par. 3. Acetone, acetone oil, and ethyl methyl ketone, 25 per centum ad valorem.

Par. 4. Alcohol: Amyl, butyl, propyl, and fusel oil, 6 cents per pound; methyl or wood (or methanol), 12 cents per gallon; and ethyl for nonbeverage purposes only, 15 cents per gallon.

Par. 5. All chemical elements, all chemical salts and compounds, all medicinal preparations, and all combinations and mixtures of any of the foregoing, all the foregoing obtained naturally or artificially and not specially provided for, 25 per centum ad valorem.

Par. 6. Aluminum hydroxide or refined bauxite, one-half of 1 cent per pound; potassium aluminum sulphate or potash alum and ammonium aluminum sulphate or ammonia alum, three-fourths of 1 cent per pound; aluminum sulphate, alum cake or aluminous cake, containing not more than 15 per centum of alumina and more iron than the equivalent of one-tenth of 1 per centum of ferric oxide, three-tenths of 1 cent per pound; containing more than 15 per centum of alumina or not more iron than the equivalent of one-tenth of 1 per centum of ferric oxide, three-eighths of 1 cent per pound; all other aluminum salts and compounds not specially provided for, 25 per centum ad valorem. . . .

Par. 1458. White bleached beeswax, 25 per centum ad valorem.

Par. 1459. That there shall be levied, collected, and paid on the importation of all raw or unmanufactured articles not enumerated or provided for, a duty of 10 per centum ad valorem, and on all articles manufactured, in whole or in part, not specially provided for, a duty of 20 per centum ad valorem.

Par. 1460. That each and every imported article, not enumerated in this Act, which is similar, either in material, quality, texture, or the use to which it may be applied to any article enumerated in this Act as chargeable with duty, shall pay the same rate of duty which is levied on the enumerated article which it most resembles in any of the particulars before mentioned; and if any nonenumerated article equally resembles two or more enumerated articles on which different rates of duty are chargeable, there shall be levied on such nonenumerated article the same rate of duty as is chargeable on the article which it resembles paying the highest rate of duty; and on articles not enumerated, manufactured of two or more materials, the duty shall be assessed at the highest rate at which the same would be chargeable if composed wholly of the component material thereof of chief value; and the words "component material of chief value," wherever used in this Act, shall be held to mean that component material which shall exceed in value any other single component material of the article; and the value of each component material shall be determined by the ascertained value of such material in its condition as found in the article. If two or more rates of duty shall be applicable to any imported article, it shall pay duty at the highest of such rates.

TITLE II
Free List

Section 201. That on and after the day following the passage of this Act, except as otherwise specially provided for in this Act, the articles mentioned in the following paragraphs, when imported into the United States or into any of its possessions (except the Philippine Islands, the Virgin Islands, and the islands of Guam and Tutuila), shall be exempt from duty:

Schedule 15

Par. 1501. Acids and acid anhydrides: Chromic acid, hydrofluoric acid, hydrochloric or muriatic acid, nitric acid, sulphuric acid or oil of vitriol, and mixtures of nitric and sulphuric acids, valerianic acid, and all anhydrides of the foregoing not specially provided for.

Par. 1502. Aconite, aloes, asafetida, cocculus indicus, ipecac, jalap, manna; marshmallow or althea root, leaves and flowers; mate, and pyrethrum or insect flowers, all the foregoing which are natural and uncompounded and are in a crude state, not advanced in value or condition by shredding, grinding, chipping, crushing, or any other process or treatment whatever beyond that essential to proper packing and the prevention of decay or deterioration pending manufacture: *Provided,* That no article containing alcohol shall be admitted free of duty under this paragraph.

Par. 1503. Agates, unmanufactured. . . .

BIBLIOGRAPHICAL AIDS

The emphasis in this and subsequent volumes in the Presidential Chronologies series will be on the administrations of the presidents. The more important works on other aspects of their lives, either before or after their terms in office, are included since they may contribute to an understanding of the presidential careers.

The following bibliography is critically selected. The student might also wish to consult **Reader's Guide to Periodical Literature** and **Social Sciences and Humanities Index** (formerly **International Index**) for recent articles in scholarly journals.

Additional chronological information not included in this volume because it did not relate directly to the president may be found in the **Encyclopedia of American History**, edited by Richard B. Morris, revised edition (New York, 1965).

Asterisks after titles refer to books currently available in paperback editions.

SOURCE MATERIALS

Harding has received relatively little attention from historians and biographers. Part of this neglect can be attributed to the mediocrity and stagnation of his Administration and his concomitant reputation as one of the nation's lesser presidents. There is also the ambiguity or dearth of information about many of the events of his scandal-studded Administration. His widow was long believed to have destroyed all of his personal papers immediately after his death. Four decades passed before the existence of some 350,000 papers of his years were revealed and made accessible to scholars.

These Warren G. Harding Papers—all that Harding had kept in his possession—are at the Ohio Historical Society in Columbus, Ohio. Nine hundred document boxes of material include the executive office files from his presidential years as well as private, political and business correspondence from the 1890s through 1923.

Also in the society's manuscript repository are the papers of Harding associates Frank E. Scobey, Malcolm Jennings, George Christian and Charles Sawyer, and biographical materials collected by Charles E. Hard, Ray Baker Harris and Cyril Clemens. A microfilm edition of the Harding and most of the related collections was due to be completed by December 1969 and available for sale and/or interlibrary loan by spring of 1970.

BIOGRAPHIES

Adams, Samuel Hopkins. **Incredible Era.** Boston, 1939. This fluidly written biography does not show Harding in any great depth. Nevertheless, it presents a lively interpretation of the political life of Harding's times.

Chapple, Joseph Mitchell. **Life and Times of Warren G. Harding.** Boston, 1924. A portrait by a newsman whose travels with the President included the trip to Alaska immediately before Harding's death.

Russell, Francis. **The Shadow of Blooming Grove.** New York, 1968. The best treatment of Harding, based on extensive research into material that included the newly available papers of the Ohio Historical Society. The "shadow" of the book's title reflects the author's belief that Harding's life was greatly influenced by recurring implications that he had Negro ancestry. Because of a court injunction obtained by a Harding descendant, the author used dashes to represent excerpts from Harding letters to Carrie Phillips.

Sinclair, Andrew. **The Available Man.** New York, 1965. This was the first work to appear that was based on the Ohio Historical Society papers. It does not, however, measure up to the Russell biography.

SPECIAL TREATMENTS

Britton, Nan. **The President's Daughter.** New York, 1927. An account by Harding's mistress of their affair, leading to the birth of a child.

Daugherty, Harry Micajah, and Dixon, Thomas. **The Inside Story of the Harding Tragedy.** New York, 1932. This is largely a defense by Harding's Attorney General of his role in the Administration. He gives his version of events, but without any substantial supporting facts.

Means, Gason B. **The Strange Death of President Harding.** New York, 1930. A distorted and sensational so-called inside view by an adventurer who had been an assistant to the FBI chief, Burns.

Stoddard, Henry L. **As I Knew Them.** New York, 1927. A newsman's recollections.

ESSAYS

The best of the encyclopedia essays on Harding is that of Allan Nevins in the **Dictionary of American Biography**.

Bagby, Wesley M. "The 'Smoke-Filled Room' and the Nomination of Warren G. Harding," **Mississippi Valley Historical Review**, Vol. 41, No. 4 (March 1955), 657 ff.

Bliven, B. "Tempest Over Teapot," in **American Heritage**, October 1965, 20 ff.

Duckett, K.W., and Russell, Francis, "Harding Papers: How Some Were Burned; and Some Were Saved," in **American Heritage**, February 1965, 31 ff.

Holbrook, S.H. "In Praise of the Harding Era," in **Lost Men of American History**, 320 ff.

Thompson, C.W. "Harding," in **Presidents I've Known and Two Near Presidents**, Indianapolis, 1929, 325 ff.

White, W.A. "Harding," in **Masks in a Pageant**, New York, 1928, 389 ff.

----. **Ohio State Archaeological and Historical Quarterly**, Columbus, 1943. Vol. 52. 260 ff.

"NORMALCY"

Allen, Frederick Lewis. **Only Yesterday.** New York, 1931.

Bates, J. Leonard. **The Origins of Teapot Dome.** Urbana, 1963. Traces the battle between conservatism and progressivism that underlay the major scandal of the 1920s.

Bernstein, Irving. **The Lean Years: A History of the American Worker, 1920-1933.** Boston, 1960.

Daniels, Jonathan. **The Time Between the Wars.** Garden City, 1966. Revealing glimpses of major figures of post-World War I America.

Faulkner, Harold U. **From Versailles to the New Deal.** New Haven, 1950.

Fleming, Denna F. **The United States and World Organization, 1920-1933.** New York, 1938.

Ginger, Ray. **The Bending Cross; A Biography of Eugene Victor Debs.** New Brunswick, 1949.

Hicks, John D. **Republican Ascendency, 1921-1933.** New York, 1960.

Leuchtenburg, William E. **The Perils of Prosperity, 1914-1932.** Chicago, 1958.

Love, Philip H. **Andrew W. Mellon; The Man and His Work.** Baltimore, 1929.

Moos, Malcolm. **The Republicans.** New York, 1956.

Nevins, Allan. **The United States in a Chaotic World, 1918-1933.** New York, 1950.

Noggle, Burl. **Teapot Dome: Oil and Politics in the 1920s.** New York, 1962.

O'Connor, Harvey. **Mellon's Millions; The Life and Times of Andrew W. Mellon.** New York, 1933.

Odegard, Peter H. **Pressure Politics, the Story of the Anti-Saloon League.** New York, 1967.

Paxson, Frederic L. **American Democracy and the World War, III, Postwar Years: Normalcy, 1918-1923.** Berkeley, 1948.

Schriftgiesser, Karl. **This Was Normalcy.** Boston, 1948.

Slosson, Preston. **The Great Crusade and After, 1914-1928.** New York, 1930.

Soule, George. **Prosperity Decade: From War to Depression, 1917-1929.** New York, 1947.

Sullivan, Mark. **Our Times, the United States, 1900-1925, VI, The Twenties.**
New York, 1935.

FOREIGN POLICY UNDER HARDING

Adler, Selig. **The Isolationist Impulse; Its Twentieth Century Reaction.** New
York, 1957.
Ellis, L. Ethan. **Republican Foreign Policy, 1921-1933.** New Brunswick,
1968.
Feis, Herbert. **The Diplomacy of the Dollar: First Era, 1919-1932.** New
York, 1966.
Leopold, Richard W. **The Growth of American Foreign Policy.** New
York, 1962.
Parks, E. Taylor. **Colombia and the United States, 1765-1934.** Durham,
1935.
Perkins, Dexter. **Charles Evans Hughes and American Democratic States-
manship.** Boston, 1956.
Pusey, Merlo J. **Charles Evans Hughes.** 2 vol. New York, 1951.
Rippy, J. Fred. **The Capitalists and Colombia.** New York, 1931.
Sprout, Harold and Margaret. **Toward a New Order of Sea Power.**
Princeton, 1940.
Sullivan, Mark. **The Great Adventure at Washington.** Garden City, 1922.
Tate, Merze. **The United States and Armaments.** Cambridge, 1948.

THE PRESIDENCY

Bailey, Thomas A. **Presidential Greatness: The Image and the Man from
George Washington to the Present.** New York, 1966.* Bailey rates
Harding somewhat higher than have earlier critics.
Binkley, Wilfred E. **The Man in the White House: His Powers and
Duties.** Revised ed. New York, 1964.* Treats the development of the
various roles of the president.
Brown, Stuart Gerry. **The American Presidency: Leadership, Partisanship,
and Popularity.** New York, 1966.*
Burns, James MacGregor. **Presidential Government: The Crucible of
Leadership.** New York, 1966.*
Corwin, Edward S. **The President: Office and Powers.** 4th revised ed. New
York, 1957.* An older classic.
Cunliffe, Marcus. **The American Heritage History of the Presidency.** New
York, 1968. A recent interpretation by a competent authority.
Haight, David E. & Johnston, Larry D. **The President: Roles and
Powers.** Chicago, 1965.* Essays on the presidency by both presidents and
other experts.

Israel, Fred L., ed. **The State of the Union Messages of the Presidents. 1790-1966.** New York, 1967. Contains introduction by Arthur M. Schlesinger, Jr.

Kane, Joseph Nathan. **Facts about the Presidents.** Revised ed. New York, 1968.* Useful, with complete information on the President's family, nominating conventions, and cabinet appointments. Includes comparative as well as biographical data about the presidents.

Koenig, Louis W. **The Chief Executive.** New York, 1964. Authoritative study of presidential powers.

Laski, Harold J. **The American Presidency.** New York, 1940.* A classic.

Roseboom, Eugene H. **A History of Presidential Elections.** New York, 1964.

Rossiter, Clinton. **The American Presidency.** 2nd ed. New York, 1960.* A standard treatment by an outstanding authority.

NAME INDEX

TITLES IN THE OCEANA
PRESIDENTIAL CHRONOLOGY SERIES

Reference books containing Chronology—Documents—Bibliographical Aids for each President covered.

Series Editor: **Howard F. Bremer**

GEORGE WASHINGTON*
edited by Howard F. Bremer

JOHN ADAMS*
edited by Howard F. Bremer

JAMES BUCHANAN*
edited by Irving J. Sloan

GROVER CLEVELAND**
edited by Robert I. Vexler

FRANKLIN PIERCE*
edited by Irving J. Sloan

ULYSSES S. GRANT**
edited by Philip R. Moran

MARTIN VAN BUREN**
edited by Irving J. Sloan

THEODORE ROOSEVELT**
edited by Gilbert Black

BENJAMIN HARRISON*
edited by Harry J. Sievers

JAMES MONROE*
edited by Ian Elliot

WOODROW WILSON**
edited by Robert I. Vexler

RUTHERFORD B. HAYES*
edited by Arthur Bishop

ANDREW JACKSON**
edited by Ronald Shaw

JAMES MADISON*
edited by Ian Elliot

HARRY S TRUMAN***
edited by Howard B. Furer

WARREN HARDING*
edited by Philip Moran

DWIGHT D. EISENHOWER**
edited by Robert I. Vexler

JAMES K. POLK*
edited by John J. Farrell

Available Soon

JOHN QUINCY ADAMS*
edited by Kenneth Jones

HERBERT HOOVER*
edited by Arnold Rice

ABRAHAM LINCOLN**
edited by Ian Elliot

GARFIELD/ARTHUR**
edited by Howard B. Furer

* 96 pages, $3.00/B
** 128 pages, $4.00/B
*** 160 pages, $5.00/B